THE LIMITS OF VIOLENCE

Lessons of a Revolutionary Life

By Élan Le Vieux
as Told to Ira Chaleff

THE LIMITS OF VIOLENCE
Lessons of a Revolutionary Life

Ira Chaleff Publications
A Division of Ira Chaleff Consultant
PO Box 663
Front Royal, Virginia, 22630
United States

ISBN-13: 978-1500258160
ISBN-10: 1500258164

Available on Kindle and other devices
through Amazon Kindle Direct Publishing
ASIN: B00OYR0FLO

Web: www.irachaleff.com

Spanish Edition:

LOS LÍMITES DE LA VIOLENCIA
Lecciones de una vida revolucionaria

© 2012 Ira Chaleff – Todos los derechos reservados
ISBN-13: 978-1456365417
ISBN-10: 145636541X
ASIN: B00KM2RWWU

TRANSCRIBER'S NOTE

The manuscript for this book was completed in all-important aspects before September 11, 2001, a day the world changed. As an American, I had to ask myself if I was still comfortable supporting a project that expresses sympathy for revolutionaries. After letting the question sit with me for some time, I have decided to go ahead with the project and release this book. But I feel compelled to explain why.

At no point did I fully agree with Élan's perspective. Why should I? His life, as you will see, was so different than mine. He lived in times and places in which one did not have the luxury of intellectually agreeing with or opposing events. The events were one's life.

To a degree, since September 11, such events have become part of my life, too. This has forced me to sharpen the distinctions that can and must be made between revolutionary movements and terrorist acts. I need to be absolutely clear about my own position.

It is courageous, and can even be considered a moral duty to resist and seek to change, by whatever means, regimes that brutalize their citizens and suppress legitimate opposition. This is the central point made by the founders of the United States in the Declaration of Independence. In contrast, using terror against the civilian citizens of a regime, regardless of one's assessment of that regime, is either an act of depraved disregard for human suffering or an act of extreme desperation that undermines the moral authority the perpetrators claim for their cause. Nothing in this book condones depravity, everything condemns it. And everything in this book supports retaining the moral authority of legitimate efforts to throw off oppression.

I was originally drawn to this project by my intense revulsion of the tactics used by rebels in Sierra Leone in the 1990's. How anyone could amputate the arms and legs of children in the service of any cause left me emotionally devastated and morally outraged! I felt compelled to respond and began looking for an effective way to do so. This initial impetus raised the deeper and central question of why do revolutionary movements too often become as oppressive as the regimes they seek to replace.

I am extremely grateful for having discovered Élan and benefited from his reflections on revolution. His voice crystallized and articulated many of the feelings I had been experiencing. Élan's goal was to help future generations of revolutionaries and would-be revolutionaries create a better life for their compatriots by learning from the mistakes and successes of the movements in which he was involved. While I shared many of Élan's ideals in my youth, I gave them up for more pragmatic pursuits in life. Pragmatism has its rewards but leaves a hole in one's sense of moral commitment. The prospect of being able to capture and record Élan's perspective was immensely attractive and paralleled my imperative to respond to the horror in Sierra Leone. The events of September 11 only make this truer.

Like all of us, Élan's views are deeply influenced by the experience of his generation and century, both of which are now gone. Revolutionaries at the beginning of the 21st century and beyond may find his reference points, and the assumptions that emerge from them, outmoded. Good. This shows that humanity is evolving. At the aftermath of last century, while some revolutionary groups like the Zapatistas in Mexico seemed to generate new models of revolution that inherently avoided the pitfalls Élan identifies, most still emulated older models. Zapatistas success at creating a new order was limited. A decade later, the powers of social media seem to even more profoundly enable the early stages of revolution to be accomplished with minimum violence. Nevertheless, the regimes they install have not always themselves been good stewards of the power they have won. I believe many of the lessons Élan learned about the healthy and unhealthy transition of power through revolution are transferable to new revolutionary frameworks. Those who are committed to overthrowing oppression need to pay attention to Élan's experience and advice if they are to be better custodians of justice than the regimes they are struggling to replace.

I am reproducing Élan's words as faithfully as possible. It was hard at times to do this as ideas poured out of him like a gushing artesian well. I have done my best to organize his thoughts. You will see that I have presented the stories and poetry he recited in italics to distinguish them from what he describes as his essays to fellow revolutionaries. In the years that I worked on this project, Élan found a place in my consciousness where he resided as a teacher and guide. His voice went with me as I tended to the necessary tasks of living. Throughout our conversations, I was deeply impressed by Élan's regard for principled revolutionaries. I hope my efforts to convey his thoughts are of use to those committed to recreating the world.

Ira Chaleff, 2001

TABLE OF CONTENTS

INTRODUCTION

I shall only reveal to you my nom de guerre – Élan. Now they call me Élan Le Vieux – Élan the Old. I am a very old man, having lived more than a century. I am either 102 or 104. When I was born, birth certificates were more of a fluid as document than they are now. You could always bribe the local record keeper to issue altered certificates for different purposes – to show that you came from this region or that, to show you were older or younger in order to evade conscription into the army, or to obscure your race or tribe that might be a barrier to your career. I've had a few birth certificates, a few different passports, too. So it is hard to know exactly how old I am.

But I have lived a very long time and I have seen much of the turmoil of the last century. There sure was enough to go around! I managed to move around the world and get assignments in some of the hottest trouble spots. I enjoyed throwing my hat into the ring when I saw a good fight going on. I always enjoyed giving a hand to the underdogs if they had a chance at overthrowing a bully. I hate thugs and bullies. There are enough of them to go around, too.

I am not going to reveal to you which fights I was involved in. Not yet anyway. You might not agree ideologically and I don't want to alienate you over what's now history. I want you to get to know me a little first. Then I'll say more about where I've been and what I think of this or that revolution. I want to first demonstrate to you that I have some useful things to say. I figure that if I'm going to say them, I'd better say them now. No phony birth certificate will keep me alive much longer. It doesn't matter to me what your ideology is. If you believe in it deeply, I think you'll find a thing or two that I've learned helpful to you.

Let me be clear. I am not just writing a book about revolution. I am writing to revolutionaries. No one, except other political revolutionaries, writes books to revolutionaries. Yet they should. Revolutionaries are among the most important people in the world. If they are successful, they will transform their societies, for better or worse. If they are unsuccessful, they will continue to struggle for years, sometimes generations, for such is the nature of revolutionaries. Unless they are exterminated or placated, they will continue to struggle. How they choose to conduct their struggle will lift up or degrade their people, will ease or exacerbate the suffering that made the revolution necessary. This is why I want to write to you. I hope you will be patient and accept an old man's gift to you.

At times when you are reading, I think you will say, "Who is he kidding? He's no revolutionary!" In part, you will be right. I have grown old and in many ways soft. But that does not mean I was less a revolutionary than you when I was twenty or thirty, or even fifty! I remember the years when the revolution burned in my soul like a hot coal! The dream of a new world! No, not the dream, the absolute certainty that we would bring it into existence! And that our way was the only way to bring it into existence! This hot coal is now in your heart. That is good. It must always be in someone's heart if the world is to become a just place. But you should be a little curious as to why it does not burn as hot in my heart any longer. If you are lucky, you will also live past thirty, fifty, or seventy. If you learned why the fire in my heart cooled, perhaps you will be able to keep the fire in your heart as bright and fierce as it is now. That is the story this book will tell, if you will read it. But let me speak for a moment to those who pick up this book out of curiosity, who may not be revolutionaries or who are tentative in their leaning towards revolution.

Revolutionaries are frightening people. They frighten those who maintain the order they are challenging. They frighten those who live in that order, even if they are its victims. And they frighten those who are in non-revolutionary situations and watch the action from the safety and comfort of their homes.

Therefore, unless one is a revolutionary himself, it is not acceptable to speak with understanding or sympathy for the revolutionary. It has been a long time since I have held a gun. I live with people now who are not revolutionaries and who have no use for revolutionaries. I will tell you how this came about later. Meanwhile, I will probably be denounced by the few remaining friends I have for speaking sympathetically of revolutionaries, for seeming to approve of the violence of revolutionary methods. But what does an old man care? Truth is more important than reputation. Eventually, reputation will catch up even if it's from the grave.

I think it is necessary that people understand and honor the place that the revolutionary has, though they may fear and deplore the means he chooses. They may even deplore the ends the revolutionary seeks and still honor him! Why? Because whether the ends are correct or mistaken, they are a response to conditions that compassionate individuals and groups should not condone. At least the revolutionary is acting, while others are sitting around on their soft behinds doing little or nothing.

I will admit to you and my revolutionary friends that I have come to abhor violence. I have seen far, far too much of it and all of it together has added up to very little good. At the same time, if the revolutionary is opposing a regime that uses violence and torture to repress its people, then I am certainly supportive of his aims, and cannot condemn his means.

But, to my fellow revolutionaries I must at the same time say that I fear that violent means will only replace and perpetuate the violence the revolution opposes, as has happened so often. Each time this occurs, it betrays the revolutionary who gave his or her blood, life, or family in the great cause. I want to draw this danger forcefully to your attention, for you do not deserve to be betrayed and, therefore, you must not contribute to that betrayal.

But I want to also speak with those who fear revolutionaries, who label you and dismiss you before understanding your cause and the legitimacy of your aims. I have lived many places in my life. For some time now, I have lived in America. Given my history, I never imagined this is where I would probably die. Don't dismiss me because of this. You'll understand when I've told you more about my life. For now, just accept the fact that I am here in what my old comrades called the "cesspool of greed."

I prefer to call America "the land of contradictions." Americans are taught from a very young age to revere their first president, George Washington, the "father of his country." Though they know he was a revolutionary leader, the general of a revolutionary army, they sanitize this in their minds. They do not think of him as a bloody revolutionary. They see him sitting on a horse, or freezing at Valley Forge or crossing the Delaware River in a boat. They don't see him leading his men into battle against the government they have forcibly rejected, muskets blazing, holes being torn in men's chests. Yet their country was born in just such a revolutionary war.

Americans, the people of short memory, love their Declaration of Independence but forget that in the eyes of the government of the day, its signers were committing treason. They revere Thomas Jefferson as the philosopher of their revolution but forget that after the revolution was won, he did not entirely disown its means. Jefferson still counseled that a little rebellion now and then is healthy and that governments should not be too harsh in suppressing it. For it is a tenet of the Declaration that government must serve the people and, when it does not, when it becomes repressive, people have an inherent right to rebel.

This is one way in which America makes me feel sick. There are others. But this is the one that makes me most sick of heart. Of all people, Americans should have understood the precious right to fight against oppressors. Instead, they forgot this. In my day, they stood behind United Fruit when they should have been standing with the brave freedom fighters everywhere in South America and Central America. They made a choice of economic interests over justice. This is the contradiction at the heart of the American ideal. Even in places where they did not have what they refer to as "vital interests", they undermined the freedom fighters. What irony! Out of greed and out of fear of their global enemy, they drove the best political minds and hearts of the century into their rival's arms and never understood they were doing this! There was nowhere else to go! America had rejected her legitimate children!

Was the American Revolution the only "good" revolution? Maybe Americans think so, but you and I know better. There have been many noble revolutionary efforts against regimes unspeakably worse than the British were to their American colonies. I have seen more than a few in my time. I have known –I'll even go so far as to say that I have loved– many good men and women who lost their lives fighting brutal oppressors and organized thugs. But I have also seen revolutions go wrong, do more harm than good. That is part of what people fear. After living a century you learn some things that can change this. I want to write to you about these things. They are important for you to know if you are to be successful. That is why you should read this and keep reading even when there are times you think I have gone soft.

Some have said that progress is made by small numbers of people with an idea to which they dedicate their lives. Revolutionaries go further, as they are willing to lose their lives for the idea. Therefore, it is more important that a single revolutionary think about the issues in this book than it is for a thousand non-revolutionaries to do so.

The revolutionary will think about these issues deeply, will struggle with them to determine if they support revolutionary ideals or if they are insidiously counter-revolutionary. He, or sometimes she —if she can make the macho men listen— will discuss them long into the night with comrades. They will argue over these ideas. It will be a very serious matter as to whether they should integrate the ideas into their revolutionary thinking or reject them. If the individual revolutionary determines the ideas contain values that will protect the revolution, he will act with courageous determination to teach them within the revolutionary community.

If you are one of these individuals, I have no doubt that at times you will encounter fierce resistance. The ideas in this book are poorly written. I waited too long, my thinking is labored, and I repeat myself too much. Nevertheless, these ideas threaten the power of authoritarian leaders, whether they are in the regime or the revolution. It will take courage to speak for the ideas in this book. But, if you are a committed revolutionary, or contemplating throwing your support behind a revolutionary group, it is vital that you discover if the leadership can tolerate honest revolutionary dialogue to help them make important decisions. Believing passionately, arguing vigorously, acting decisively, and requiring loyalty once decisions are made, are one thing. Suppressing dissenting views is something else entirely. It is a sign of paranoia, of the inability to share power with others. If the revolution isn't about power being shared equitably, what is it about? If the leadership is paranoid, it will become more so once the revolution is won.

INTRODUCTION

As unthinkable as this thought seems to you now, leadership that won't tolerate dissent will use the power it has amassed in ways that betray the revolution. It is almost impossible to let yourself imagine this when you are giving everything you have to support a movement and its leadership. Yet, read history. This happens with lamentable frequency. Why would a revolutionary give five, ten, or twenty years of his life for that? Far better is to find out now, to confront now, whether this will be a genuine revolution or merely a change of power wielders. Far better is to make one's move now to influence the character of the revolution or to abandon it if it will not be a revolution towards greater human dignity and justice. And, if you are the leader, far better that you learn how to proof yourself up against the abuse of power, that terrible disease to which all leaders are susceptible, than to be placed by history in the gallery of rogues you so detested as a young revolutionary idealist.

I wish that I had learned this sooner myself. It is one thing to die for the revolution. That is a very real possibility you accept when you go into it. As they say here, "It comes with the job." It is quite another thing to live your life serving the revolution only to "wake up" twenty years later and discover that you gave your life to something that wasn't worth it, to something that you now have to reject. It is a terrible moment in one's life to feel like such a fool, though you were not really a fool.

This has happened to thousands of revolutionaries and it is a great and terrible shame. It is important to understand how this can happen and how you can avoid this happening to you. That's what I am writing to you about. How to be guarantors of a true and worthy revolution. Note this well or you might mistakenly think that I have nothing to offer you. You already have a theory of revolution, a strategy, and revolutionary models. I am not a great thinker. I do not pretend to compete with these or to offer you a better blueprint. What I offer you is a way to guard against your own blueprint failing. The structure you build must become a wonderful new edifice, not a worm-eaten, corrupt bureaucracy, or worse, a prison.

There are always many more non-revolutionaries in the world than revolutionaries. Perhaps the ratio is ten thousand to one. There is a lot that non-revolutionaries can learn from revolutionaries that would be good for the world. Some will assume this book is a metaphor for non-revolutionaries to shake up and change their organizations or professional fields. I have lived in America for a while and America is very big on this. They sell management books by referring to them as the secrets of this historical figure or that one. Genghis Khan, Abraham Lincoln, General Patton, Gandhi, Machiavelli, Jesus. Such an assortment! I have watched American management with fascination because they produce so much wealth. I have seen that managers may be agents of change but they are hardly revolutionaries. They always work within the existing system.

Nevertheless, I suppose they can learn from this book. Because they, like revolutionaries, can and often do commit excesses and then rationalize their actions. Their words sound hollow and hypocritical as they fire ten thousand people from their jobs and say that it is to improve "global customer service" when no one believes this crap.

But this book is not a metaphor. It is written for genuine political revolutionaries and those contemplating the hard life of revolutionary activity. The stakes for revolutionaries are infinitely higher than the stakes for any manager. But like the manager, the revolutionary leaders' words will sound hollow if they talk about "serving the people" but act only to consolidate their own power.

I have written this book to give you a chance to reflect on the values that determine how you conduct the revolution. When you have little to eat or wear, when you do not see your family for months or years, when you are hunted and desperate, or stymied at every attempt to light a revolutionary fire, you do not normally have the time and frame of mind to reflect on your values and conduct, and their accord or discord. But a great revolution demands this. It demands this of the revolutionary and the revolutionary demands this of his or her leaders.

I have written a short poem for you about this. Writing poetry and stories are things I have done to keep the years interesting and to capture something to leave before I move on. This is for you.

THE DEED

When the heart's blood runs beneath the wound
and on cold ground you lay dying
will you have been true to what you knew,
will the deed have been worth the trying?

Will right thought and acts be braided tight
to bind the shattered heart?
Will the sinews have the strength to lift
those left to play their part?

Will you regret the times you could have done
your deeds some other way?
Or will you think of times your acts held trae
to the words your lips would say?

In all the world there are far too few
who will take on friend and foe
And to each say "yes" when yes is right
and when not, be steadfast in their "no!"

It is my wish, and it may well be my dying wish, that this book is translated into every language in which revolutions are being fought. Let the revolutionary veteran, the recruit, the candidate and the critic come away better for having wrestled with these ideas.

Élan, 2000

PREFACE:
What is Revolution?

Make no mistake, much human progress is not revolutionary. It is evolutionary. The great forward motion of human culture depends on the stability of a non-revolutionary environment for the accumulation of knowledge and resources and wealth. Look around and you will see this everywhere. Ignore for a moment the unjust distribution of these things or the tawdry uses to which they are put. Just observe the depth and complexity of the culture all around you and recognize that it has been learned and developed and refined over centuries.

It is a serious error to take the wealth of a culture for granted, to overlook the hundreds of crafts and professions, the tens of thousands of artisans, the scores of professional societies, the institutes of learning, the laws and customs that have made all this possible. It is why prolonged civil wars are so destructive. They wipe out the fruits of centuries of culture and leave the countries in which they are fought impoverished. It is why revolutionary purges are devastating; they so weaken the cultural pool of knowledge. Long periods of evolutionary progress are necessary and desirable even when they are imperfect and inequitable. I am sorry if you do not want to hear this. It is the way things are.

But, periodically, a culture goes as far as it can go without a revolutionary change, whether the revolution is scientific, social or political. The culture is stagnating, resisting all efforts to move forward, to include new ideas and greater numbers and classes of people. It refuses to reassess what is important.

At such points, civilization is rescued and advanced by those who can think and act outside of the existing ways of thinking and acting, by those who are willing to turn the existing ways on their ear and put themselves at great personal risk should they fail or have their timing wrong. Revolutionary leaders, and the small numbers of people who support them early in the revolutionary effort, make huge differences, all out of proportion to their numbers. They are following Archimedes' words and finding a place to stand and a big enough lever to move the world.

You and I are particularly interested in political revolution, though I sometimes think scientific revolution trumps us in making the real changes in the world. I'll confess that it bothers me to think that the materialistic engineers who invent an electric light or a radio or a computer might be having more real effect on the world than the brilliant social thinkers I have known in my life.

In any case, I keep up with social and political movements. I read newspapers in three or four languages a day, depending on what I can get my hands on. As I read about the world, thankful that my eyes are still good enough to do this (though my eyeglasses are as thick as telescope lenses), I am struck by how many opposition movements there are on every continent and how many of them are armed. They all call themselves revolutionary groups but I wonder how many are truly revolutionary?

This will get us into a philosophical discussion of what is a revolution. And I do not want to bog down too much in such a discussion. I already told you that I no longer hold a strong brief for any one philosophy. Those days are past. What I do hold to is an underlying principle: a political or social revolution must in some way free people from some form of oppression.

But if we accept this premise, overthrowing the oppressive order is at best only a third of the measurement of success. Another third is replacing it with a new, less oppressive order that allows people to participate in their own governing. And the final third is doing a better job than the old system of satisfying the legitimate needs and wants of the people in whose name the revolution struggled.

We see an example of this now in South Africa. The world rejoiced that the revolution against apartheid succeeded and rejoiced again that, to this date, it has replaced the old order with a more just and opens, if still flawed order. Now South Africans and the world wait to see if the new order can change the entrenched economic effects of decades of apartheid. This will be the final determinant of success.

But this measurement of a revolution's success is oversimplified because it does not sufficiently take into account that there is always more than one group involved. There is always a group that is in power that is oppressing in some way other groups that do not have as much power. What is the responsibility of the revolution to the group it deposes from power? And what to other groups competing with it for power?

Clearly, the deposed group will have less of some things than it had before. It may have less political power, economic power or cultural power. There is no way that it can still have all the power it previously had relative to the groups that staged a successful revolution. But it is my contention that if the deposed group now becomes as oppressed as the victorious group once was, a revolution has only occurred in the narrow sense, not in the broad sense.

Yes, you could say a revolution has occurred. What was once on top is now on bottom and vice versa. The stuck wheel has turned. It has revolved. But it is my contention that in true revolution the wheel doesn't turn half a cycle and stick again, reversing the top and bottom. In a true revolution the wheel spins more freely giving all the spokes a chance to continuously reach the top.

This requires a new way of thinking and behaving on the part of the victorious revolutionaries. They cannot simply become the new top. They must become something different. They must become the force that keeps the wheel spinning so there is no top and bottom, so that all groups have a share of power. In that dynamic state they have reduced the oppression of all groups and the pressure for counterrevolution.

If one race was on top, now both races have a chance to live with some dignity. If one tribe was on top, all now have the opportunity for success. If secularism reigned, now religion can flourish by honoring all choices of religious practice. If the wealthy lived on the backs of the downtrodden they can still live decently, while the poor are no longer held down in the mud.

I know. This is beginning to sound like a fairy tale. But I do not think revolutions must not have happy endings. My point is that a true revolution does not just replace roles of who gets to oppress whom. It behaves differently. It reduces oppression broadly. That is not too much to aspire to. That is not too much to ask to be incorporated into the true definition of revolution.

No, it is not too much to ask. But it presents a very great challenge. Revolutionaries are desperate people. Desperation is a source of their power. Usually, they have little or nothing to lose. Occasionally, we see this rule broken by exceptional individuals who have everything to lose but lead or join the revolution anyway, because it is the right thing to do. Then they, too, become desperate as they have incinerated their bridges and there is no going back except to prison or a firing squad. But desperation is also the source of a revolution's excesses, and the justification for unjustifiable actions. Desperation is the soil from which unforgivable acts arise, and in which they are denied and buried.

The great task of the revolutionary is to preserve the values of human dignity that spawned the revolution, despite the threat of losing the revolution and losing one's own life. This is almost an unbearable standard by which to ask a human being to live. It is the standard for which churches award sainthood. Yet it is the standard to which a revolutionary must aspire in order to avoid betraying the revolution.

Some say the true revolution must occur within oneself before it can occur outside in the world. While this by itself is insufficient for creating a revolution, I have also come to believe it is true. If we engage in revolution with only models of force and oppression in our minds, we risk falling back on these to get the job done. Yet these have been burned into our minds. How can we not fall back on them?

We need to find better models or, if we have none, somehow become better models ourselves. This is the heroic task, the make or break of a revolution. Che struggled to be a good model. He sometimes fell back on the ruthlessness used by oppressors, but I think this was out of great fear of losing everything that had been won. Once he became more confident that the Cuban revolution would survive, he showed signs that he would respect those he fought for, and even those who were part of the old order, if they gave the new order a chance.

Mandela is the best model. He used violence without becoming violence. He used violence only as long as it was the necessary tool and laid it down as soon as it was not necessary. By transforming his anger (the internal revolution) and by trading the gun for the ballot and the levers of administrative power at the right moment, he gave his country the best chance for successful revolution in the meaning of the term I have explained and that I hope you share with me. Whatever models Mandela drew on, he became an even greater model for others.

Now I've shown my hand. You can see the bias in my political philosophy. While, like many revolutionary thinkers, I believe it is the historical context that makes the revolution possible, I also believe that it is the individual and his or her actions that make a difference to the revolution's success or failure. You are that individual to who I am writing.

PRELUDE:
My Life

Let me tell you a little about myself, before I go on. You are listening to me preach at you, so you deserve to know a little about who is doing the preaching.

I will not be as specific as you may like. After so many years of hiding, of disguising my identity, of changing my papers, I am not comfortable being too specific about myself. And it is far too late to change that.

Perhaps, if someone sat with me for days with a tape recorder and asked me many questions, the pieces would come out and could be fit together. But I am not important and no one will bother to write my biography. I am fortunate that this young man is willing to listen to what I have to say and help me write my thoughts down in some intelligible order. That is good enough.

I was a witness to many of the important events of my century, which is now passed, and I knew many of the important people who shaped those events. Some I knew well, others a little, and still others I knew by reputation only, through overlapping acquaintances or comrades by whose side I fought. It is one of the points of pride of my life that I knew so many, one way or another, even if I never was smart enough, or ruthless enough, to become a central figure myself. History will forget me, but you may remember me if you find and read this book.

You must remember how old I am. It is hard to imagine, even for me. Imagine to have been born in the century beginning with 18__, even if I just squeezed into it. To still be alive is an accomplishment not many can boast of. Especially when you have had as many close calls as I have had!

But, I tell you, the details of my biography are not important. What is relevant is that I came by the revolutionary life honestly. From the earliest days that I can remember, my house was filled with men who talked of politics and revolution. We lived in the usual way for those days – several generations together, in a large, simply furnished house, or clustered in a few houses near each other. When I was seven or eight, the age one can begin paying attention to such things, my grandfather lived with us. He was almost seventy years old, which was very old for those times. Relative to how long most people lived; it was as old as I am now. But he was still vigorous, more so than I am, except on a few mornings when I feel strangely young again.

You must realize that this would put him of age when the 1800's were only half over. This was a volatile time. Bolivar and Jose de San Martin had passed from the scene in South America, but his father knew and talked of them. In North America, the abolitionists were creating a stir, pushing to extend the American Revolution to the vast numbers of blacks who, to its shame, had been excluded from the new social order. John Brown was one of the people my grandfather greatly admired. In Europe, Karl Marx was already writing and advocating class warfare. But my grandfather's personal preference was the indefatigable revolutionary, Giuseppe Mazzini. Mazzini worked for forty years, pamphleteering and inciting insurrections. He worked tirelessly to create a consciousness of national identity around which Italy could transform itself into a nation and wrest control away from foreign powers and warlords, much like China would do in the next century.

Our house was a little larger than the houses of our neighbors, so it became the nightly meeting place where my grandfather and his friends, and just as often his adversaries, talked half through the night. They argued about who was right: Marx or Mazzini. Mazzini had concluded that Marx's theories would only result in worse poverty and the substitution of one ruling class for another.

Regardless, Mazzini was my grandfather's hero for a variety of reasons. The man was a saint. What little money he had he always shared with his comrades who were in worse need than he. Every penny he raised went to the cause, never to himself. He took risks all the time, always trying to get something started. Garibaldi had the army and the fame, but he was so cautious, always protecting himself and his image, missing opportunities Mazzini tried to seize.

My grandfather honored Mazzini because he could continually do three things at once. First, he could hold a clear vision of a new society and incessantly fight for it, despite countless setbacks that drove lesser men into despair and inaction. Second, while holding that pure vision, he could make realistic compromises to achieve the essence of it, when achieving the full vision was not pragmatic. Third, while holding his own pure vision, he could honor those who held different visions, competing with them for the minds of his countrymen, rather than needing to destroy them. My grandfather would tell me that other revolutionaries could do one or another of these things, but he had not met the man who could do all of these.

Naturally, by the time I was old enough to listen to his conversations with friends and adversaries, they had long stopped talking of Mazzini. The nights were filled with arguments over Trotsky and Lenin, the Mensheviks and Bolsheviks, the virtues of democratic socialism versus dictatorship of the proletariat. Little did I understand at the time that these were the most crucial issues of our century, that they would fatally shape the nature of revolution for the rest of the millennium. I only knew that these were the kinds of things men talked about at night, every night, and that some went off and acted on them.

I took this talk very seriously; in fact, I took it literally. At the ripe age of seventeen, I announced that I was leaving to join the revolutionary struggle. My father blanched and my mother broke down weeping. She wept for three days, but on the day I actually left` not a muscle on her face quivered.

She had come to accept that this would be my life, that it would not be the life of the last century, but the life of the new century. That it would not be the life of talking and arguing the nights into dawn, but a life of action. She could not be angry with me because she would have to be angry at my father, and at her father and at his father. She knew that such anger would be misplaced, as it was not the will of the fathers that the world was in its wretchedly unjust condition. If she was to be angry, it would have to be at the world itself, at the way it was put together for the cruel benefit of the few. What good would that do in her position?

So, as I began the life that is ending by my writing this book to you, she said good-bye to me with a stoicism I have not seen again to this day. It is strange to be a hundred years old and still miss your mother.

CHAPTER I:
Anger and Violence

Hard Life:
Anger at Injustice

Life is hard for many people. It is only when we perceive that life is being made unnecessarily and unconscionably hard by the actions of the ruling class or clique that we feel the stirring of revolutionary impulses.

It is an easily observable fact that life is hard, and that it is harder for some than for others. How we interpret this fact leads to a revolutionary frame of mind, or not. We may perceive that life is unbearably hard for reasons that do not trace to the policies or actions of a ruling group. This is not a revolutionary situation though it may produce a crisis of faith or a crisis of cultural will to endure the hardships.

If people are religious, they seek to understand extreme hardship through their understanding of God and the design of this universe. They wrestle with how the God they worship can permit suffering of such intensity or scale as that which they witness. They pray for an understanding of the purpose of suffering. They struggle to perceive its redemptive value. If they cannot find redemptive value they would be compelled to rebel against God, or their concept of God. Indeed, some have lead revolutions that banished God from their country, to the degree that this is possible.

Whether or not we are religious, we seek to understand and reduce the causes of suffering in the natural world. This is a great hallmark of our humanity. We search for cures for diseases that leave children deformed or dying in agony. We build levees to hold back storms, dig sanitation systems to purify drinking water, organize fire brigades to save trapped families. We develop social and economic theories to explain what we are observing and unearth clues on how to change it. We do so for selfish reasons and for unselfish reasons. It is in our nature to seek to prevent or reduce suffering.

And then there are those who, in grim contrast, add to the suffering that exists in life. Out of greed, out of fear, out of a lust for power, out of mental derangement, there are those who act in ways to increase suffering in the world. The rest of us recoil. Even if we turn a blind eye out of fear or preoccupation or helplessness, we recoil.

One of the functions of civil society is to organize ourselves so that we collectively have the power to stand up to those who add to the suffering of others. This is a prime function of government. But what are we to do when the government itself has become the perpetrator, or the protector of the perpetrators of suffering? When it is so dedicated to maintaining the favorable position of one segment of the population that it will not use the collective resources it has gathered to reduce the suffering and elevate the lives of other segments? When corruption and greed and psychopaths have entered the government itself and it is now the greatest purveyor of suffering? Inevitably, in this situation, the government will use its power to maintain the intolerable status quo. Who will try to change this? To stand up to injustice and thuggery? It is not easy to stand up to the organized might of a government. As you know, more have died trying than can be counted.

Those who stand up may come from among the injured or they may come from —and this is one of the redeeming characteristics of human nature— those who witness the injuries and cannot abide them. In either case, they start from a point of great sorrow and anger, from an emotional recoil sufficient to cause them to act. They act reflexively as a crowd or deliberately as an individual or group. In one way or another they act.

But anger itself is directionless. It lashes out. It tries to destroy and often it destroys the wrong things or even destroys itself. In this condition anger is politically impotent. Politically potent anger is always linked to an analysis of injustice and its causes. It becomes what is called in English, outrage. This is a highly directional form of anger. Instead of rage that is indiscriminate or that turns inwards on oneself or one's own group, it is directed outward at the external sources of the injustice. Outrage has potency.

By their outrage and the determination that grows from it, individuals are transformed into activists. They will attempt to use all the legitimate power the society affords them to redress the wrongs they have risen against the press, the petition, the ballot if it exists, the meeting, and now, the Internet. But when these are denied or fail them, and the repression continues, what are they to do? Where are they to go?

It is from this juncture of suffering, outrage and repression that the revolutionary is made. The true revolutionary. Not the "revolutionary" who is being used as a pawn of a hostile power or as the tool of arms merchants or diamond or drug cartels. Not these patsies who are being cynically used to support a despicable agenda. These patsies had better wake up and confront the truth of how they are being used!

But even the true revolutionary must be alert. By themselves, sounds of anger and outrage are strident and cacophonous. They hurt the ears and disturb the mind. By themselves they do not attract the support a revolution requires. When someone does nothing but rant and shout, people shut their ears if they can. The jagged sounds of outrage must be linked to hopeful descriptions of freedom and wellbeing. To sounds of harmony that, deep within themselves, people know can exist if they would be allowed to exist. The cacophony and the harmony together form a compelling tension that will attract and hold the attention of oppressed people. They will listen and then they will add their own voices. They will become a great choral work which, like all music, seeks to resolve the tensions within itself.

The true revolutionary is singing the canary's song in the mineshaft. It is a song of alarm and a song of beauty. He has become hyper-alert and what he observes is that the injustice has gone on too long and his people are suffocating. They are dazed from asphyxia and he is singing furiously to wake them up while they can still be woken, while there is still power in their limbs to knock a hole in the walls and let in the air they have been denied. That is the revolutionary's alchemy: to transform this great anger he feels into a life-saving song that will command the attention of his people and move them to act.

To Become a Revolutionary?

As I have said, anger alone is not enough to make a revolutionary. Anger alone makes an angry person. How is a revolutionary developed?

Revolutionaries are rarely made overnight. It usually takes many years and wrenching experiences to change the thought patterns that accept the status quo into which one is born. The individual must stop accepting the definitions of normality imposed by the culture. He or she must negotiate several existential transitions. I am using big words but let me explain. Some who read this may be contemplating a revolutionary life. They should understand the path before committing themselves.

Each individual's journey to social consciousness and action is unique but there are common crossroads. The first crossroad occurs when the pre-revolutionary individual achieves the awareness that he exists as a distinct entity. (When I say "he" you will know that I mean "or she" as well, but it is too difficult for me to keep saying this so you will please bear with me). He is not just the package of customs and parental shoulds and shouldn'ts into which he is born. Yes, he is indelibly part of his heritage, his class, his ethnic group. But he is also an independent agent who can make choices about how to interpret his heritage and whether to conform to it or not. He is free to embrace his heritage more fervently than his family and friends or reject it and look to other sources of identity. In my adopted land, Martin Luther King Jr. used the pulpit of his father to transmit a transformational message of racial integration. Malcolm X rejected this heritage for the platform of Islam from which to create a radical Black consciousness.

Once the individual is clear that he exists as an independent agent within his cultural context, the second crossroad he arrives at is to discover what kind of person he wants to be in relation to the world. It may seem that he has no choice, that he is who he is. There is truth in this but it is not the complete truth. There are layers to his personality and there are roles and limitations that are imposed on him. The revolutionary journey requires that he examine these critically and decide which to accept and which to challenge. He may need to reject some aspects completely, or reject them at this time and learn later how to incorporate them into his identity. The full picture of who he is and who he can be is larger than that which the world is permitting him to believe. As the revolutionary philosopher Frantz Fanon observed, we are free to reject the categories through which others seek to imprison us.

The emerging revolutionary must also form an understanding of the world. Not as it superficially appears but of how it actually works. He must seek experience and question what it means. Why are things the way they are? How did they get this way and what holds them in place? It is healthy to not swallow the first interpretation he hears but to seek and weigh several interpretations for himself. As he forms his own synthesis he then needs to ask what is he prepared to do about his new understanding. Nothing? Something? What specifically?

At some point he must stand up and declare who he is. This sounds so easy once the threshold has been crossed. It is, in fact, a huge step. It took Che riding his motorcycle across South America to work this out for himself. There were so many expectations placed on him from which he had to free himself before he could declare who he wanted to be.

If the individual has reached the point of knowing who he wants to be the third crossroad is to survey the range of choices available to achieve this. There is always a spectrum of groups that he can join or affiliate with. Each will approximate in varying degrees the identity he has declared for himself. None are likely to be a perfect fit. Which will most closely match his vision and temperament? Or, should he form his own group? Is he enough of a leader to formulate a unique vision and attract others to it?

He must open his eyes wide at this point and understand the differences in the range of groups and strategies to choose from. Some choices will have consequences that will affect his entire life, or even cost his life. Or the lives of others. He must question his values and his tolerances. He must question his maturity and ability to evaluate the available choices.

It is possible that he should first choose a reformist path. Though this path is an anathema to revolutionaries, it is nevertheless true that sometimes systems can be radically changed through steady efforts from within. He may at least test this path even if he later rejects it. This choice will also allow him to test himself and his motives.

Choosing either a reformist or revolutionary path requires courage as, by this point in the journey, there will be great internal and external pressures for and against each. He will be wooed by groups that each act from their own interests. They will make compelling arguments that are irresistibly seductive in their desire to include him as one of them. It is not wrong for these groups to create this attractive picture of their cause. All energetic groups do this. But this alone is not sufficient reason to agree to assimilate philosophically and physically into that group.

I have learned in my life that sometimes the revolutionaries are right and sometimes the reformists are right about what strategy is the correct one for a given time and place. Embark on a reformist path when there is no political space in which to operate and you will prolong your people's suffering and seal your own death warrant. Embark on a revolutionary path when there is political space available and you will unnecessarily endanger thousands. Embark on this path when the winds of revolution have not sufficiently gathered and you will have achieved nothing, but will have ruined your life. It is not easy to discern the path out when you are in the depths of the forest but this means that, more than ever, you should keep your wits about you and head in a carefully considered direction.

There is no shame in exploring alternatives to revolution. There are enough things in life to be ashamed of. Caring sufficiently to try several paths for creating a better world is not one of them. But neither can you dither in a Hamlet-like paralysis. The oppression you witness requires you to act.

But this is the third and critical crossroad: to which group or movement to give allegiance? There is always a spectrum of groups that he can join or affiliate with. Each will approximate in varying degrees the identity he has declared for himself. None are likely to be a perfect fit. Which will most closely match his vision and temperament? Or, should he form his own group? Is he enough of a leader to formulate a unique vision and attract others to it? The choice made here holds great implications as it is the first crossroad that demands a public act, even if for security reasons it is a secret act. But a choice must be made or the individual will float in a no-man's land

At this point a new journey will begin. A journey rich with comradeship, with purpose and meaning and, at times, confusion. The individual's declaration of loyalty to a group almost always cuts him off from belonging to other groups and, in a revolutionary situation, from the society at large. Now, if he is not to drift as a pariah to all groups, he must strengthen his bonds with the group he has chosen and earn its trust. His physical and social survival becomes inextricably intertwined with this group. Rejection comes to seem unthinkable, even fatal.

It is precisely because the choice has such import that the would-be-revolutionary should give it all the thought it deserves. The decisions made at this crossroad are often irreversible. Once made you put your whole life into your mission. Before they are made you think carefully and consciously. If you are standing at this crossroad, perhaps you will find my experiences relevant to your decision making.

Violence:
Its Uses and Limitations

Violence and revolution. The Siamese twins. Joined at the smashed hip. The liberals deplore violence. They only point to the acute violence with which you, the revolutionary, are associated, not at the chronic violence against the people who lack basic food and medical care and clean water. The people die of malnutrition and diarrhea while their rulers live on delicacies and drink cognac and go to the best clinics.

But why the rejection of violence? Why do the liberals make such a stink about it?

There is violence everywhere in the world. On the land. In the sky. Under the sea. The animal kingdom is divided between the killers and the killed. Predators tear their prey apart. Males destroy each other in their drive for leadership and mating rights. Ants organize themselves into armies.

The plant kingdom is no less violent, just slower. Kudzu chokes forests. Algae choke rivers. Poison berries and mushrooms kill those who eat them. Toxic vines welt the skin.

Look at the Earth itself. The violence of the tectonic plates as they grind over each other, shaking buildings into rubble, suffocating thousands under cement and crumbled bricks. The volcanic eruptions that bury towns in ash or lava and abruptly end the life of whole villages. The typhoons that drown and the tornados that smash.

Even the stars that songwriters idealize are nothing but violent chain reactions, thermonuclear furnaces spewing jets of gas a million miles into space. Their birth is violent, their life is violent, and their death is violent.

Bringing this back to Earth, I am sitting here in my violent, adopted country, where people kill each other hourly with the millions of guns they own. In the face of all this, am I going to preach to you about the evils of violence? Another hypocrite who makes arguments against your brand of violence while neatly justifying other brands of violence?

I'm not that stupid. After living a hundred years, I'm not that stupid. I would lose you as a reader. I don't intend to lose you. You are too important. Too much rests in your hands. So I will not preach to you against doing what the rest of the universe does. You have as much right as the rest of the universe. But there are cautions. Cautions that you should heed.

As you know, it is just as true that the world runs on cooperation as on conflict, on collaboration as on violence. Your own movement would not exist without cooperation between individuals and cells, between the civilians who support you and your regulars, between yourselves and your allies. Without cooperation, food could not be distributed to your people, intelligence would not find its way to you, and these new websites you use would not be available.

Of the two forces in life —violence and cooperation— cooperation will take you many times further than violence. All of your goals, all of your ability to radically transform human life is dependent on your ability to cooperate and to get many groups and individuals to cooperate with you.

Violence must be reserved for those who are using violence to destroy you. Far too often violence is misused as a means of obtaining, of all things, cooperation! Listen to this carefully for it is a great and central confusion. You cannot obtain cooperation through violence! You can obtain short-term compliance. That is all. Is that what you want? Is that what you need? Not if you are to create a genuine revolution! You need long-term, freely given, spirited cooperation.

Almost all great abuses of revolutionary power are caused by this confusion. The rest are caused by the desire for revenge or by psychopathic individuals gaining power. The revolutionary leader who would see his or her revolution create a new life for the people in whose name he is fighting, must avoid this confusion. You cannot violently obtain cooperation.

Let me tell you a story. I promised you I would tell you stories. These stories are more interesting than my ranting and will make the long nights in your camps a little shorter.

The Elder and the Revolutionary

Jose de Antigua sat in the bushes out of sight of the trail. He was well camouflaged. The animals could smell him and took care to avoid him. But people walked by unsuspecting his presence.

Jose was waiting for the right person to walk by. Last week he had spoken with Emmanuel Sanchez, the village elder. He had spent two days in Senor Sanchez' village, almost all the time sitting with him, eating with him, talking together, pleading.

Jose had come on a mission. His mission was to secure the help of Emmanuel Sanchez. His village, Santa Doria, was near a pivotal crossroads used heavily by the army. Jose wanted Emmanuel to have his people report to them on the movements of the army in great detail. Sanchez was unwilling to persuade his people to do this. His reasons were varied.

First, he did not want to put his people at risk. There were rumors that the army had burned another village to the ground when it suspected that the villagers had supplied food and information to the rebels. Second, the government had promised him a new well and his people needed the well so badly. Third, he was not yet sure that he trusted the rebels. Emmanuel had lived a long time. He had heard many promises. Few had been kept. The rebels promised they would help Santa Doria but, when the time came, Emmanuel knew he could not count on their help. Not yet. They had not yet proved themselves trustworthy.

Jose had pleaded with Emmanuel. Then he became angry. He stood up and shouted and paced around the small hut where they were talking late into the night. He called Emmanuel many disrespectful names that elders should not be called. Then he began to threaten. If the army would burn Santa Doria for helping the rebels then the rebels would burn Santa Doria for not helping them! Take your choice old man. Jose would not make it an easy choice.

When Jose began to rant the old man withdrew into a place inside of himself that was impenetrable to others. It was a place he had gone to for many years when strongmen had threatened him. There was always a strongman threatening. Some called themselves governors, others generals, others drug lords, bandits or rebels. He did not care what they called themselves. They all behaved the same.

There had been one who had been different. Many years ago. He had called himself a rebel but he spoke differently. He understood the hardships Emmanuel's people suffered. When he could, he brought them tools that he had obtained on raids, to make their work easier. He did not ask them for things. He simply wanted to understand their needs. Emmanuel found himself giving this rebel commander things he did not ask for, things that did not come easy for the village to give, but things that the rebel leader would surely need.

Jose did not know this story. Nor did he understand Emmanuel, what he was made of and to what he responded. When he was in Emmanuel's village he had seen Emmanuel with his youngest son, a boy of ten. He had seen the affection with which they spoke to each other or touched each other. Jose sensed that here was a way to get to Emmanuel, to secure his cooperation. His love for the boy was a vulnerable spot.

Jose waited at the side of the road. He had learned that Raoul, Emmanuel's youngest son, passed here on his way to and from school. He would be with some other children, but not with adults or armed guards. After nearly dozing off, he awoke as he heard laughter. He peered carefully through the bush and saw Raoul joking with a friend no older than Raoul himself.

Jose leaped out of the bush brandishing two guns. He shouted at the boys to fall down or he would shoot out their stomachs. They froze in terror, practically unable to fall on the ground as ordered. Jose helped them with a heavy shove each. He began yelling not to move, not to move an inch or he would ensure they never moved again.

Jose tied the boys' hands and dragged them back into the bushes where he had been waiting. He blindfolded and gagged them and had them march a couple of hours to a secret camp he had set up, deep in the hills. There he tied each boy to a tree, still blindfolded. He was not a man to waste many words. He told Raoul he needed to send a message to his father. Raoul began to say that he would try to help. Before the words were out from his mouth, Jose had taken a straight edged razor and with a controlled and vicious slash, he had removed the small finger from Raoul's right hand, which had been lashed to the tree.

Raoul screamed. His friend froze at the shrieking sound Raoul made. "Shut up" Jose roared, "or you will lose another!" Just as suddenly as he had made the cut, he produced a flask of whisky and poured some over Raoul's bloody hand. Raoul screamed again. Jose ignored the scream this time and quickly and expertly taped a bandage around the stump of Raoul's severed finger and stanched the bleeding. Raoul passed out from the shock of what had happened.

Jose wrapped the finger in another piece of gauze and turned his attention to Raoul's friend. He shoved the amputated finger in a pocket of the friend's shirt and untied him.

"I am leading you back to the road that will take you to your village. When we get near the road I will loosen your knots and disappear back into the bushes. You will be able to free yourself in several minutes. You are to return to your village and go straight to see Emmanuel Sanchez. In your pocket is a gift for him. You will tell him that he is to send you back tomorrow with the information I requested. I will expect such information every week. If I do not receive the information I will send him another gift, and another. If there is any effort to trace you to my camp, Raoul will die."

The boy followed Jose back to the road. Jose removed his blindfold and loosened his knots, then disappeared back into the bushes. After a while, the boy undid his knots and ran to find Emmanuel Sanchez.

The next day the boy returned to the spot to which Jose de Antigua had ordered him. Jose anticipated a wealth of information on army moves. He knew the old man would not betray him to the army as he hated the soldiers as much as he himself did. He simply had to put as much pressure on the old man as the army put on him and he would cooperate.

When Jose saw the boy he grabbed him by his shirt and hauled him into the bushes. He pulled a sack over his head to obscure his vision and tied a rope to his waist. Then he half-led, half-pulled him back to the little camp.

Raoul was again tied to the tree to ensure that he did not run off while Jose was away. Now Jose tied the other boy to a tree again.

"Well" he said to the boy "what does Emmanuel have to tell me?"

"Look in my pocket" the boy replied.

Jose dug in the boy's pocket. There was a note and something wrapped in gauze. Jose tore open the gauze. He briefly gasped. There was another finger wrapped in the gauze. An older finger, with gray hairs and a yellow fingernail.

The note read: "Senor de Antigua. You will find a reciprocal gift to the one you sent me. It is my own little finger. Every time you send me a piece of Raoul's body I will send you a piece of mine. In the end we will have lost Raoul and you will have lost the entire village of Santa Doria."

Violence versus Force

"The deep summons the deep"
— Latin proverb

I will start this subject with a question. Who is the real revolutionary? Who is a fake? It seems evident, but it is not always that easy to know.

It seems obvious that the revolutionaries are people with weapons who are willing to use them to overthrow the oppressive regime. But maybe they are not revolutionaries. Maybe they just want to replace the existing regime with their own. Maybe they would use the same oppressive tactics to maintain their own power once they have the reins.

On the other hand, men without guns in their hands do not appear to be revolutionaries. If they are protesting the practices of the regime without guns in their hands, they seem to be hapless reformers. By refusing to allow themselves to use the same tools of violence that the regime freely uses, they appear to be playing into the hands of the regime. Nothing will fundamentally change.

I certainly believed this. It took a lot of bitter experience for me to reconsider this view. I'll fill you in on some of that experience later, but for now let me stick with the ideas in this chapter. I just want you to know I did not change my views sitting on my padded ass In a soft armchair in a comfortable room. I changed them on the front lines, like you, with my ass exposed.

In some situations there may be alternatives to armed revolution, in others there may not. Non-revolutionaries always throw Gandhi in your face as an alternative. But the situation Gandhi faced was very specific and in other situations he would simply have had tanks roll over him. Nevertheless, I have come to believe that alternatives should always be exhausted before committing to violence. It always requires force to unseat an oppressive regime, but not necessarily violence. Passive resistance as a strategy is misnamed. It always requires active resistance to unseat oppressive forces.

Using force without violence requires supreme courage. When you march, or organize, or pamphlet, or boycott, or stand in front of a tank, you will be beaten and jailed and fired on and sometimes murdered.

Arson, rape, lynching, torture and exiling will all be used against you. The first thing to get very clear about is that using force without violence requires every bit as much courage as armed struggle.

Force is always preferable to violence where the situation leaves it possible to use non-violent force. Force does not blow off the legs of children or orphan them by the thousands. When you forcefully and aggressively use all non-violent means at your disposal, you automatically occupy the politically and morally high ground from which you can attract attention and support.

I will go out on a limb and tell you that in certain circumstances you can substitute surprise, boldness and humiliation for acts of terror, with much greater results. Yes, you heard me right, humiliation.

History demonstrates to us that in almost all cases when revolutions are successful at overthrowing the oppressor, the regime was already severely weakened and primed for collapse. Though seeming fearsome and strong, it was rotten at the core and unsustainable. If this is true, a case can be made that, rather than fomenting panic through acts of terror, it would be just as effective to make a laughing stock of the regime.

Bear with me a moment while we let our imaginations run wild. Imagine creating any of the following events:

Tying up a dozen of the regime's elite forces, leaving them clothed only in lace panties and telling whatever press outlets to which you have access, where to find them.

Taking the uniforms you removed from the elite forces, filling them with helium balloons and releasing them in the capital to show how full of hot air the regime is.

Chaining the guards of a detention center to a wall with the chains they use to torture prisoners, videotaping the transfer and distributing it as widely as you can through foreign news services or on this amazing communication means people call the Internet.

These thoughts make me chuckle. It is good to laugh once in awhile. Your imagination can run even freer than mine. I do not mean to make light of serious matters. But mockery is a powerful weapon you should not overlook or dismiss. If it's headlines and public opinion you are after, I guarantee you these tactics will be effective. Besides, the oppressors have humiliated people for decades. It is satisfying to give to give them a taste of their own foul medicine.

Of course, such tactics presume that you have a strong political arm that can get your message out. And they presuppose enough political space in the degenerate regime to make use of such tactics. But, let me tell you, I have learned that such unexpected tactics can be as or more powerful than tactics the regime expects from you. Besides exposing the weakness of the regime and emboldening its many detractors, they have a similar effect to the mafia leaving a horse's head in someone's bed as a warning. It demonstrates that you can do what you want and it is only your current self-restraint that keeps you from doing more. That can change.

Like every tool, there are uses and limits to non-violent force. The challenge is to become skillful enough at the use of the tool so that it does as much work for you as possible. When it can do no more, even in skilled, committed hands, you reach for other tools. When the other tools have done their work of heavy lifting and hammering, you return to the finer tools for the shaping, smoothing and finishing.

Mandela is the greatest example of the balanced use of force and violence in my lifetime. I suppose this makes him revolutionary of the century in my book. If only I were in a position to grant awards!

For decades the African National Congress maintained a policy of non-violence. In the face of provocation, harassment and defeat, they adhered to this policy. You could argue that they adhered to it too long, but that is hindsight. They utilized the spaces left open to them by the surviving framework of the British legal system to press their case. As long as those pockets existed, they were occupied and utilized as platforms.

But the pockets shrunk. And decades of occupying them produced no change. So Mandela, this very principled man, reluctantly came to the conclusion that the path of non-violence could no longer be walked when violence was routinely being perpetrated against his people.

The great irony of Mandela is that he was one of the first ANC leaders to call for the inclusion of limited violent tactics in their strategy, but, because he was imprisoned before he personally became involved in armed struggle, and remained imprisoned for 28 years (!!), his own hands remained clean of violence and the world thinks of him as a great peace bringer. He did bring both peace and justice. But, as much as the world may wish to forget this, he also steadfastly refused to renounce violence while the oppressive regime used violence to sustain its immoral rule. His words still ring in my ears: "It is always the oppressor, not the oppressed, who dictates the form of the struggle." Of course, he did not mean that the opposition does not have the power of choice, but eventually it will have to select means to respond to the options the oppressor leaves open.

So even in the final stages of the struggle, when the government was negotiating with the previously banned ANC, Mandela refused to renounce the use of violence until the government did likewise.

But what kind of violence? Great care was given to target the violence against military installations, against the symbols and instruments of the police state, against leverage points in the economic infrastructure. This is completely opposed to tactics of random violence that terrorize populations based on the premise that if you can generate enough terror the enemy will capitulate or be overthrown. To the contrary, these tactics just as often stiffen resistance. And when random and widespread violence becomes a strategy it is self-defeating in the long run. Why?

You see, there is a simple secret to all political leadership that Mandela knew. This may be the most important "secret" I can share with you. You must hold your people together. In every country the people are divided into North and South, or rich and poor, or Muslim and Hindu, or light skin and dark skin, or Hutu and Tutsi, or native and immigrant. The bigger the country the more ways in which they are divided. And it is the primary duty of a political leader to hold them all together. For as soon as he does not, there is civil war with its ruinous consequences.

If you perpetrate unforgivable violence against groups of your countrymen in your quest to gain power, you will not be able to heal the breaches with the groups you have violated and win them over. The memories of violence are indelibly burned into their minds and they, in turn, burn them into the minds of their children. Sooner or later they will rise up against you. Maybe in this generation. Maybe in the next. But they will rise. If you are to avoid civil war and the failure of your vision, you must limit the violence you use to gain power. If you must use violence, use just enough, just enough.

In South Africa, it was never assumed that victory would occur through defeat of the South African security forces. They were too powerful. Direct military confrontation could only result in millions of casualties over many years, a ruined country, and a Pyrrhic victory for one side or the other. The goal was to make the country difficult to govern if government continued to use brutal and degrading policies against the majority of its people.

This is not true, of course, for all revolutions. Each is unique as to its circumstances. It is sometimes assumed that military victories are possible. This may be so. But in the end, it still comes down to working out how to live with those you have defeated. The greater the violence perpetrated in reaching this point, the less chance there is of sustaining a new order that doesn't rely on the same oppressive methods you fought against. If you rely on those methods, the oppressor has won. He has transformed you, instead of you transforming him.

Basic Acts

The shit came long, clean, urgent.
He was grateful it was clean.
Messy shit in the battlefield can be one thing too many,
sapping the will to keep going.

A twisted road had led him to this battlefield
with his pants down around his ankles.
He did not regret this road
and only wished it had an end that he could reach.

The road was supposed to go to some place completely new.
He desperately hoped it could find that place
because he was tired and in danger of not caring where it ended
as long as it reached there soon.

The will to keep going was everything
in a world that was designed to erode it by throwing small insults
at you every day
in between the large injuries.

He wiped himself with leaves.
He yanked up his trousers
and cinched his belt.

These basic acts would have to occur
whether the war ended or not,
wherever the road wound,
and whenever it stopped.

Some things are continuous
even during radical change
and their reality cannot be forgotten.

Young Revolutionaries

I know I am lecturing you but that is all I have time for. I cannot engage with you in dialogue as I would like. It's hard enough for me to whisper with the young man who is helping me capture my thoughts. Even he sometimes cannot hear me. So now, as a very old man, I will talk to you about the very young.

You will often attract the young to your cause. They bring their idealism and energy and have little fear of losing things. In their zeal, they will move towards excess. Do not encourage this and do not allow this. Though their excess may help you in the short run, it will hurt your cause in the long run. If you win, one day these young people will become part of society again, and one day they may help run that society. Do not allow them to become thugs as they may remain thugs and corrupt the society you long to build.

If you see a young person engaging in excess, laughing at the suffering he is witnessing or causing, slap him once very hard so he remembers the slap and the look in your eyes forever. Tell him it is never his role to enjoy the suffering of others. Sometimes he may cause the suffering of others as a byproduct of what he is trying to achieve, but he should never enjoy it. If he is to be a man and a worthy revolutionary, it would be better for him to cry at the suffering than to laugh at it. His role is to help people, not to make them suffer. If the young person is a woman, remind her that a woman gives birth to life and it is her special role in the world to protect children and to be concerned for the welfare of the adults the children need to raise them.

Sometimes these young people will cause suffering without having meant to do so. That they did this is so painful to them they must deny it is painful and turn it into a joke, a cruel form of play. When they have done this once, they must continue to do this in order to keep out the reality of the pain they first caused.

When you encounter young people the first time that they have caused suffering you must grab them by the arm and shake them. Tell them that you understand how bad they feel about what they have done. That you know they did not mean to cause such suffering and that they wish they had not caused so much suffering. That they are good and caring people and it is terrible that in revolution and war good and caring people hurt other people. This way they will know that it is okay to feel the pain of having caused suffering and they will not need to block it out by contorting the causing of suffering into a false and hideous virtue.

Think about what I am saying! If you think about it, you will realize that I am saying you must do what you can to create men and women who are the opposite of those who serve the regime! The opposite of those who can torture and kill others with sneers on their faces, indifferent to their pleas. This is truly revolutionary!

If you are a revolutionary commander you already take care to indoctrinate your young recruits in the values of the revolution. Beware as they observe every gap between what you say you value and the actions you take. They know that what you do is what you really mean. Use your responsibility to the young to refresh your own commitment to the values you claim to live by.

If you are a confidante of the commanders, pay attention that they have not themselves forgotten how to feel the pain their people both receive and inflict. When they have seen too much, when they have felt too much, when it becomes unbearable to feel more, they are in danger of shutting off their feelings. I say danger and I mean danger. They and the people they are rescuing and their young protégés and the whole revolution are in danger. The individual who shuts out feeling, who cannot bear the pain of feeling, becomes capable of perpetrating unfeeling acts, terrible acts, because they can no longer feel the consequences of those acts in others' lives. They become models of insensitivity and cruelty.

If your comrade stops feeling, recognize the danger. Take him aside and sit around a campfire or a rock or a table covered with oilcloth and get him to talk about the suffering he has seen. Loosen him up with some drinks if he needs this. Have a few shots together. Laugh together, curse together. Then get him to talk about the family members he saw killed, the men who were dragged away and disappeared, the women he could not save from being raped, how angry he felt and, underneath that, how helpless he felt. And yes, get him to talk about the people he made suffer. For the sake of us all, get him to cry, get him to scream, get him to moan in self-pity for what he has been through! And hold him, hold him and rock him and tell him it is okay, that you understand, that it is important to cry and scream, that this is not weakness, that it is the source of strength. But also, that it is the source of his humanity. Help him retain his towering anger but do not let him bury it.

When he feels his anger, help him direct it at the injustices. But do not let him direct it towards the perpetrators of those injustices, for then he will become a perpetrator. A true revolutionary cannot become a perpetrator. In your refusal to let your comrade become a perpetrator, you will also save yourself from becoming a perpetrator, and all the young builders of a new world who are in your charge.

Tell your young charges, and by your deeds show your young charges, that if they seek a just society they must conduct themselves justly. If they seek a society in which honest people, educated or poor, will be cared for even as great changes are thrust upon them, they must treat people in ways that care for them during the revolution. If the revolution does this and fails, it will not have failed. It will continue to live in the hearts of the people and rise again another time. If the revolution succeeds, it will truly succeed and not replace one oppressive regime with another.

Encourage your young volunteers and conscripts to take effective action but to always weigh their choices. Yes, their actions will need to be dramatic. They will need to leverage their scarce resources by doing the startling, the unexpected, things that confuse and tie up large quantities of the regime's resources and that hit them where it hurts. Teach them to choose, all else being equal, the actions that cause the least suffering. If the revolution is for a true cause, whatever its particulars it is trying to reduce unjust suffering. Whenever possible, select tactics that honor this. They may be powerful and shocking but they must not be hideous. Depend on revealing the oppressors' horrors for your headlines, not on promulgating your own. Do not let your legacy be another generation trained to make their countrymen suffer.

Let your legacy be young men and women who are the guardians of a better world than that into which they were born.

The Rabidly Angry

There is one last problem related to this subject that I would like to address. It is a problem faced by every revolutionary group. You will not only attract to your cause those who are angry at injustice, you will also attract the rabidly angry. The rabid, as you know, froth at the mouth and cannot be trusted. Sooner or later their disease will assume full control of them and they will attack and destroy randomly. Revolutionaries do not attack randomly.

This is a problem because you are desperate. You have such limited resources, so few hands to do so much work. You cannot afford to be choosy about who will be allowed to help you. If they are fit, can endure hardship, believe in your cause and can fight or carry provisions, you are not the government with its bureaucracy and endless, if lack luster resources. As people straggle into your cell or camp you have only one question: Are they infiltrators? Have they been sent to win your confidence and become privy to your plans and then betray you? You are always on the lookout for the rat or the provocateur. You must be. This is part of your responsibility as a revolutionary, one of your instincts that has permitted you to survive. But if they are not an agent sent in to undo you, what other reason have you to reject their support? So what if they are angry? You're angry too!

I submit to you, brave revolutionary, that you must be as wary of the rabidly angry as you are of the agent provocateur. One is unpaid, the other is paid. Either will cause you great trouble, will undermine and discredit you and your cause. Do not be tempted by the short-term use to which you can put the rabidly angry. You will pay too dearly in the long term.

The rabidly angry have been so injured that they cannot distinguish one authority from another. They deeply resent all authority, including yours. They will obey you out of fear when you can observe their actions. But they will not obey you when they are out of your sight or out of sight of those loyal to you.

"So what?" you say. "They're rebels. I'm a rebel, too." I'll tell you "so what". You will warn this rabidly angry individual to not harm the peasants whose support you depend on. A prime revolutionary principle. One day you send him out as a squad leader to ambush a military patrol that is searching for you. He comes upon a bus of migrant workers trying to get to another village where there is work. They are afraid of the military so they seem to be supporting the soldiers. He finds they gave the soldiers food and water and little pieces of inconsequential information to pacify them. The rabid squad leader decides to make an example of the migrants even if your policy is not to make examples when you are utterly dependent on the goodwill of the local people. But he is living by an internal dictate that is far more powerful than your policy, a dictate of taking out his lifelong anger on whoever riles him. He orders all the migrant workers into the bus. Then he sends a shell into the bus that consumes it in a fireball while all those inside scream until they can no longer scream. Your own soldiers look on in horror. They will never be the same. Some will find excuses to leave you. Others will become butchers themselves.

You are responsible for what your people do – all your people. It will seem that you are supporting and condoning this rabid agent of yours. Your enemies will use his atrocities to fan the flames of public opinion against you. You will be handing them the ammunition to aim at your heart. Reasonable men and women who sympathized with your cause will be turned against you by the atrocity of "your" methods. Those on the fence will jump into your enemy's camp. You say "But the government does this anyway! They manufacture stories against us! Send in provocateurs to discredit us!" Yes, but they are lying! If you let your rabid patrol leader loose, they would not be lying. Truth is one of your fiercest weapons. Will you let it drop from your grip?

It is not difficult to detect the rabidly angry. They spew venom. They talk of people being unfit to live. They dehumanize the enemy, characterize him as filth and vermin. They want to squash him and see him suffer. Or, they are very quiet. Eerily quiet. They do not speak. They glower and mumble. But if you test them with questions like, "What would you do if you had my power?" or, "What should we do with our enemies when we have won?" they will reveal their murderous intent, their desire to hurt and maim and kill. Not to redress wrongs, or create a just society, but to destroy.

What can you do with the rabidly angry who attach themselves to your cause, whether or not they are invited? You can, of course, refuse them comradeship. Throw them out of your camp and tell them to never set foot in any of your camps again. Maybe this is what you will do. Maybe this is all that you can do. But taking this firm stance also has risks and you are better off saving your risks for combating the oppressive regime. It has taken awhile to detect this rabid man's pathology. He knows things about you, your strength, you areas of operation. He may turn on you, pick at your flanks, expose your position, and act anyway in your name. If you turn him away you will have stirred up his bottomless anger and given it nowhere to go, except at you. But neither are you in the business of eliminating someone because of what they may do. You would soon become as oppressive as any regime you are fighting.

There is another possibility. There is a chance that you can transform this anger in the crucible of service. It is worth a try. You can put your arm on the rabid individual and look him in the eye. You can explain that you need men like him but not while he is so angry that he will destroy too much. You will give him an assignment that will both help the cause and purify him as a warrior. He must go to a hospital or orphanage or rehabilitation center and work with children who have been the victims of the war. Not the victims of the government, but of the war. Of the acts of both sides. He must see the price people are paying because you have decided to fight. He must understand that both sides contribute to suffering. That you are not proud of the suffering your side is causing. That your great desire is to prosecute your just cause in a way that effectively weakens your enemy's power while causing the least suffering possible.

You are assigning him the job of easing this suffering. He is to volunteer to tend to the wounded children and to their wounded parents and grandparents and help them get through this terrible event in their lives. He is to create a revolution within himself in which he can once again feel compassion, not rage. He will learn what suffering the revolution must not casually cause even if the other side lacks these scruples. He must learn how not to become the other side. Then he can return to camp to teach others.

Is this dreaming? It sounds like dreaming. But doesn't all revolution require dreaming? Perhaps you can replace the rabid man's nightmares with dreams. At least you will have tried. That's what revolutionaries do. Despite the odds, they try when others do not.

Deliverance

When faced with torture we all pray for deliverance. We pray for deliverance from the laws of physics, the laws of physiology and, at last, from the laws of morality that forbid us to acquiesce to the torturer, when the only deliverance is acquiescence.

Nguyen had been a great admirer of French culture, of Montesquieu and Voltaire, of Lafayette and Danton, of the Jacobins and the Paris commune, of Zola and Sartre, of the Marseillaise and Picasso's Guernica.

Now Nguyen had fallen into the hands of French intelligence. It was not possible for him to be naïve about the French. Experience did not permit that. But neither could he reconcile the spirit of what he once admired in French culture with the depraved brutality that was now crushing him.

For two weeks he was left in a darkened, fetid cell, no larger than a small closet, left to fend with the feces and urine he passed in the corner he allocated for this purpose. His clothes had been taken. He could not wipe his ass. His body became covered with sores from rubbing on the coarse stone of the cell. The sores turned red, then yellow before they started oozing. The process had begun of breaking him without anyone so much as touching a finger to him.

Then the beatings began.

A beating keeps its own time. Each blow is the basic unit of counting. Thirty blows to the face, the kidneys, the groin is a..., a what? A nightmare? A day? The hour before death?

What is the period between beatings? A unit of bruised agony? A unit of terror at the knowledge the respite will soon end? A unit of hope and mustering the will to live?

What calendar is used to mark a numbing series of beatings? Do thirty nights of thirty blows or sixty shocks or a hundred gaggings constitute a month or an eternity?

Nguyen soon lost count by any reckoning. Time became an enemy that existed only as a continuum of suffering. He was no longer part of a culture that knew about clocks and rest days and holidays. He had fallen through a gap in the fabric of space-time and was writhing on its barbed thread.

When does a human being begin to lose the structure that holds a personality together? When he loses the language to describe what is happening to him? When his nerves lose their conductivity but can never rest? When he is forced to watch his friends swallow their urine and pieces of their genitals because they are too willful to reveal information?

What is the period called when the beatings have stopped with no explanation and with no way of knowing when they will begin again? When the broken skin and bones knit along ragged seams? When the mind is possessed with the thought that if the beatings resume you will not be able to stand them and will reveal the information you desperately wish you never had? That your so-called strength to resist will have been as wasted as your lost teeth and your ludicrous faith.

Nguyen had been raised to endure. But he could never have imagined how much he would be asked to endure. Nor could he have imagined how the faces of his tormentors would occupy his mind. The sickening grins. The cold eyes. The grunts of almost sexual pleasure as they struck him again and again.

Whom did he hate most? The one who was most cruel, the ringleader with the crooked nose and the volcanic temper? Or the others who were not evil men and should have stopped the ringleader, but did not, night after night?

This particular night, Nguyen lay on the stone crying. Tomorrow he was sure he would break. He had exhausted any reserve of strength and all his pride. Tomorrow he would betray his friends and would no longer be proud to be who he was. He whimpered in rapid, shallow breaths as there were not enough fluids left in him to sob.

The next morning the cocks crowed as they do. Without explanation, and as suddenly as he had been imprisoned, Nguyen was freed, almost shoved onto the street he never expected to see again. The daylight blinded him. He walked painfully, tentatively. The freedom should have sent a huge wave of relief through him, but it did not. While the world he stepped into was superficially the same as that he had left, it was forever altered, forever a *place of horror waiting just around the blind curve. And he had come a razor's width from succumbing to that horror.*

In the end, we who have been tortured, come to recognize that there are only two types of deliverance for which to pray as only these can make a difference.

First, we pray not to be broken, to not let the spirit that has sustained us collapse, unable to inflate again. We pray that we will recover sufficiently to once again stand for what we remember believing.

Then we pray to not be transformed into an agent of retribution though our experience cries for this. We pray to rise above our experience and retain the will to determine how it shapes us. We pray to let our life be driven by a longing for justice not an obsession with vengeance.

Nguyen prayed while he walked away from the place of his agony. His lips moved like those of the demented. It was all he could do as he shuffled. Certainly he could not say what day it was.

INTERLUDE:
Reflection

Before I begin the next chapter, let me say a few words about the revolutionary leadership I have personally seen.

It was a very difficult century in many regards. I would never have predicted that it turned out the way it did.

The leaders that arose were large enough to leave their imprint on history. But they were not always large enough to rise above their own grandiosity.

My greatest sense of turmoil surrounds the figure of Vladimir Ilyich. Most of the world remembers him as Lenin. Of course, he used so many names.

Vladimir Ilyich was a giant. He was big enough to tame mother Russia. Big enough to begin the largest political experiment in the world. Big enough for a whole century of revolutionaries to emulate, or to use as their starting point for varying the experiment to fit the conditions of their countries.

But I fear that Vladimir Ilyich also did more than any single man to distort the nature of revolution in our century.

I watched V.I. up close and was always stunned by his intensity, his ruthlessness. It seemed to me that this must be what the revolution required and we were fortunate to have a leader of this mettle, who was not at times soft like the rest of us.

But I became confused as I watched his ruthlessness turn, time and time again, against his own comrades, his revolutionary peers. They, too, were committing their lives to creating a new world. Their voices deserved to be heard. But V.I. interpreted any deviation from his positions as a personal challenge. He draped his ire in revolutionary terms, but I have no doubt, now, that it was the challenge to his personal dominance that drove his vehement insistence that others adhere to his directives.

I could not sort out my confusion then, nor for a long time afterwards. My life was too wrapped up in "the cause". It was too important that I believe in the leadership. The voices in my head that protested against this action or that, had to be relegated to the edges of my consciousness where they would not interfere with my commitment.

People who were not near V.I. did not perceive this. His public personae was, of course, compelling. Because I had, at times, secretarial duties (well, maybe my duties were better characterized as those of a messenger or, if we had been on a ship, cabin boy) I saw what others did not. People who thought him their friend never knew that he signed their political death warrants. When they wrote for leniency or reconsideration based on the facts, they always believed others stopped their letters from getting to V.I. They could never believe the possibility that it was V.I. himself who refused their entreaties

You could say that I am placing too much importance on the personal, when it is the historical dialectic that was important. Perhaps. But these were comrades of the same ideological persuasion. Somewhere, there must be room for loyalty and justice based on an individual's actions.

What shocked me most deeply, and again I had to block all this out at the time, was that V.I. was not interested in progress or the betterment of conditions for the workers. In fact, he regarded progress as antithetical to the revolution because it might deprive the revolution of support. At the deepest level, I always assumed that we were fighting for the improvement of the living conditions of the masses of workers and peasants. It only became clear to me later that V.I. was only fighting for power. He was correct, of course, that at the core we had to change where power resided, but at the expense of betterment for people who already suffered so much? Only years later could I see that relocating the power, while leaving it completely concentrated, was not the nature of revolution that produced the results I was willing to die for.

Of course, history treated V.I. kindly and blamed all the abuses of power on Josef Stalin, the Eagle of Georgia, as he became known. But Stalin had a very good teacher. It all happened so long ago that, at times, I wondered if I had invented some of these images of Vladimir Ilyich that history didn't seem to confirm. Then I read with great interest (I never stop reading) after the USSR was dismembered and some access to the state archives was allowed, that my memories had not fooled me. Note after note of V.I.'s had been preserved, condemning his fellow comrades to forced labor, or ordering the slaughter of hundreds of peasants to make an example of this or that.

Yes, maybe I have gone soft. But the proof is in the bread pudding. Revolutions follow the example set by their leaders. Governing bodies become what their leaders allow or encourage them to become. If V.I. had used all his prestige to set a different example of how power is used, perhaps the great experiment to which we gave our lives would have turned out to have been a lasting success, instead of the grave disappointment it became.

CHAPTER II:
Revolutionary Leadership

Confusion of the Personal and Political

So, now I will continue imparting to you what I think I have learned. Forgive me if I sound pedantic. Just consider my ideas. Maybe a few of them will be important to you.

Revolutions first occur inside of us, before we fight them in the outside world. They are rarely complete inside of us before we take them outside. They form at a different pace, in a different way for each revolutionary. There is disentanglement from the belief system holding the oppressive regime in place, from the belief that it is the given order and cannot be overthrown, or that you cannot acquire the power to overthrow it.

The interior revolution is invisible. It does not bleed or smell. Those who are very close to you can sometimes see it in your eyes, in your quiet thinking, in the long walks you take to sort things out for yourself, in the hours you spend on your cot, awake but not moving. It can be very gradual, taking years, or it can happen in one moment when blinders are stripped off your eyes by a terrible sight.

It often takes on a vision within your mind of destruction: the destruction of an evil ruler, of a corrupt system, of an unjust set of rules that are brutally enforced, of a palace that houses the evil minions. This vision of destruction is powerful. It is motivating. It is also deeply dangerous. When all of your vision embraces stopping an evil, you are in danger of going insane. Visit a mental institution and listen to the inmates, listen to what they are ranting about. It is usually to stop something they feel is wrong or terrible. When you become fixated on stopping something, no matter how evil it is, you lose touch with the creative, generative side of life.

I like this word, generative. It has come to be important to me. It embraces the concept of bringing something new into the world, something beyond yourself, and leaving it for the next generation, for the world. The older you get, the more important this concept becomes to you. For me, you will understand, it has become central.

Revolutionaries must remain generative or, when they finally obtain power they use their power to stop things. They stop dissident views. They stop divergent cultural practices. Depending on the nature of their revolution, they stop religious expression or secularism. This makes a disaster, not a revolution. You can stop life for just so long and then it rebels. Your revolution is discredited and you are overthrown. What a waste.

Stopping an evil must be a subset of what it is that you want to create. The creative vision of the future is what must guide your difficult decisions and actions. What kind of society do you want? What values and policies and institutions will promote justice and engender industry and loyalty?

All revolutionaries think they have this vision. I am challenging you to be sure that you have it. To be sure that this vision is truly dominant, and not subordinate to a fixation on stopping the old ways of doing things. I have seen too many revolutionaries deceive themselves. At the core, hidden even from themselves, they wanted most to stop the old ways. They would do anything to ensure the old ways never return, even sacrifice their vision of the new way.

What you can legitimately stop are only subsets of what you are trying to create. If you want to create decent living conditions you can stop profiteering. This sequence will work. But if your focus is on stopping individual ownership, you are unlikely to create decent living conditions as a subset. The generative goal must dominate. I am getting close to treading on your political philosophy here. That is not my intention. I am concerned with your focus and approach.

If the things you want to stop or eradicate become the focal points, you will begin stopping other things. You will stop people from speaking and acting and thinking. But not everyone will stop, so you will imprison or hang or "disappear" people who refuse to be silenced, forgetting that you yourself once refused to be silenced. Then you will have become what you did not want to become. How many revolutions have done that?

Maybe the government killed your brother. Maybe it has forced thousands of your countrymen from their land. The injustice burns inside you like acid. This is your personal wound. It is an important link to the journey you are on. But it is not the journey. The journey is in the future. It is remedying the ills, creating the future. It is not retribution for the past. You will always miss your brother. No matter what happens to the forces who killed him, you will always miss him. The wound is your wound to carry through life. Perhaps you will comfort yourself with a wife and children, but it is still your wound. The revolution is the people's. Even those who were not wounded will share in it. Do not seek to heal your own pain through the revolution, though it may happen. You are fighting to heal the country's pain.

Pay attention to the difference between your inside and the outside, to the personal and the political, to creating and stopping, to the past and the future. Struggle becomes a habit, and habits cause us to cease paying attention. The true revolutionary must pay attention so he does not let the revolution become so stale that others, in exasperation, create a revolution against it, wasting the years he devoted, the blood he gave.

Pay attention to the revolution inside yourself, even as you pursue the external revolution. In the course of time you will become even more fervently revolutionary, as there is a continuous reinforcement of revolutionary belief in the life you have chosen. This is only part of the internal revolution. If it is the only one that occurs it can be dangerous.

The other part of the internal revolution must be your increased understanding of yourself. You are an instrument of the revolution. Are you a well-tuned instrument? Each of us is complex. Your revolution may emphasize how we are shaped by class struggle, or neo-colonialism, or the will of Allah. This becomes your primary belief system. You should use your belief system to take you as far as you can in understanding yourself and your role in the world. But I caution you, that there is still a need to understand what is unique about yourself. It is clear to you that one revolutionary leader is very different from another, even though they both come from the same background and share a similar worldview. In the same way, you must come to understand what is different about yourself from any other revolutionary, and how that difference can help or hurt your cause.

Whatever your cause, you are fighting for power. The internal revolution must prepare you to be ready to use power well. This is no small feat. It is one of the greatest journeys of human development. Only a few great leaders successfully make the journey. Others acquire power and use it as an extension of their personal fears and desires, and they ruin the revolution.

You have a wonderful laboratory at your disposal: the revolution itself. Observe yourself in the many different situations in which you are placed. Observe how you act and react. Compare it with others. Who uses the power they acquire to serve the common good? Who uses the power they gain for self-aggrandizement? Observe carefully what about their behavior is different from each other. Observe what is different about their behavior and yours. Learn from both of them. Sometimes the virtue of one is that he is strong-willed, and the virtue of the other is that he is thoughtful and just. Perhaps you can synthesize these in yourself and become a better, more balanced instrument.

Even as you practice to become a better marksman, practice to become a better leader by studying yourself and learning the difference between the personal and political within yourself. Che was always examining himself. It was one of the things I liked best about him. I will say more about Che later. For now, examine yourself and improve yourself. You will become a better human being and, if the revolution is successful, you will become a more trustworthy wielder of power.

Let me tell you another story. We all like stories. From the time we are toddlers and can barely understand language we like to hear stories. I'll tell you something you don't know yet: we still like stories when we are so old that we once again need diapers. When my time comes, I think I would like to drift off hearing someone tell me a story.

Tomorrow

Joseph's hand was on the trigger. Here, in front of him, was the white master. The devil who had lived for all those years in the large house on the veldt, while he squatted with his family on the pitiful plot of land allotted to him.

This was the master who had refused to drive him to the hospital when his wife was not doing well in labor. "She'll be okay. You kaffirs are a strong breed."

This is the master whose rotten system made sure he couldn't afford an automobile of his own. Who made him dependent on the master's generosity and judgment and whim. In his own judgment, his wife needed medical attention right then.

"We'll wait through the night before we decide to take her in," master decreed.

She had not lived through the night. She and her baby had died in the women's arms. Screaming until she was too exhausted to scream, bleeding until there was no blood left.

"Wives die in childbirth," the master proclaimed in the morning. "It's too bad."

Of course wives die in childbirth he screamed in his head, of course they do. But sometimes husbands can save them if they have automobiles and doctors.

He knew all the assumptions this master made. If the white man hadn't been here, there would be no hospital and no automobile to take her to the hospital. So there is no guilt on his part. How could there be?

But the white man had been here a hundred years and had made sure that no kaffirs were trained as doctors. The white man made sure that only one black man in a thousand might drive an automobile. All apparent generosity was self-serving. There was no generous sharing of cultures, only the use of white culture to dominate black culture, and eliminate it when convenient.

Now it was different. The veldt was ablaze with uprising and he, Joseph Nbule, sat with the gun in his hand. The master sat with his wrists bound, blood congealing on his scalp, the ugly wound still oozing.

For a hundred years master's people had denied Joseph and his ancestors power over their lives and their lands. Had frustrated all their legal attempts to regain a portion of that power. Had driven nails into the lid of the powder keg to hold it on, until one nail emitted a spark that blew the whole keg.

And now Joseph sat with the gun. And there was no one to stop him from using it. He could use it if he chose and repay his wife and his wife's ancestors. He did not even have to pull the trigger. He could use it to keep the master where he was, far from a hospital. He could keep him there until infection set in, and flies spawned their maggots in the putrefying flesh so he would die like his wife had died, from no access to a hospital. From the arbitrary action of one man over another.

Joseph contemplated the course of action. He could see master move beyond the ability to scream, or plead or talk the gibberish of the demented. He could feel how the great weight of his own anguish would roll over to the other side of the scales, and put things back in balance. He could hear his ancestors sigh with relief that they had been avenged. The prospect was compelling, almost demanding that it be allowed to materialize.

Joseph raised the gun and aimed it towards master. He looked master in the eye and saw him look back with fear and hate. He saw him moments in the future, lying in a pool of his own blood, as it soaked into the earth.

Joseph's finger curled on the trigger. Again, he saw the future. He saw himself burying master in an unmarked grave, so there would never be proof, so there could never be retribution. And in that moment, he saw that master would still be defining him, categorizing him as he had his whole life, this time as a murderer.

But this was not what Joseph chose to be. He would define himself from this time forward, and he chose to define himself as a revolutionary, as a transformer of society from the brutal to the just, from the exclusive power of the privileged to the inclusive power of those with social conscience.

The war continued to wage inside Joseph, as it did outside on the veldt. The muscles in his finger, at the command of the adrenaline pumping in his body and the filaments running from his brain, continued to increase the pressure on the trigger. As they reached the point of no return, he thrust his arm to heaven, closed his eyes and let come forth a scream that echoed from the deep past, all the way into the distant future, which only his children might witness.

As the bullet tore its way into the sky, the words formed from his lips. "I am not Joseph! That was the name YOU gave me. I am forevermore Andele, the name of my own people. I will follow the course of my people's future. I will never again react to the course of your people. I am free of you where it matters most, inside of my own thoughts!"

Andele whirled three times under the bright sun, the light in his eye matching the light of the world. Then he laughed, a deep, cleansing laugh. Then he cried, a deep, cleansing cry. A peace settled over him. He breathed it in and breathed it back out, sure that there was more where that came from.

Then Andele began to arrange for medical attention.

What Makes a Good Human Being?

If you are devoting your life to a revolution you must ask yourself, "What makes a good revolution?" Before you can answer that question you must ask yourself, "What makes a good human being?" Human beings create oppressive regimes. Human beings create revolutions against them. What makes one bad and the other good?

You may think you know the answer. You may think that it is obvious. You may reject my assertion and say "It is the corrupt system that is the problem and will be the problem regardless of which individuals rule it." Or, at the other end of the spectrum you may say, "It is the corrupt individual who is ruling us that is the problem and once we change him we will have solved the problem."

Do not be so sure of either answer. The interplay of systems and individuals is enormously complex. Attention must be paid to both if you are to have a successful revolution.

Your revolutionary philosophy already gives you interpretations about the system. You have a socio/economic or theocratic or racial Manichean model that helps you to understand what your people have experienced and for what you are fighting. You can tell already what my biases are and to which models I may be most sympathetic. But I have no interest in disputing your views. While they may or may not ultimately prove true, they are true at this time for you, and undoubtedly have some validity as a way of understanding the time and place in history in which you find yourself.

But I wish to caution you, and I hope you will let an old man caution you, to pay attention to the forces at either extreme –to the power of the underlying cultural structure to keep the existing system in place, regardless of your efforts to transform it, and to the power of the individual leader to abet or resist these underlying forces, and thus to create real transformation, or not.

You may say, for example, that what makes an oppressive regime are the terrible policies of taxation and land ownership, of labor exploitation and indigenous repression, of censorship and secret police. That a good regime would set up fair taxation systems and redistribute land, that it would encourage unions and honor the rights of minorities, that it would allow free expression and have fair courts and honest police. It seems so obvious.

But is it? What happens if your idea of fair taxation is different from those who will be taxed? What if they avoid your tax collectors and transfer their assets overseas and disguise their revenue? You will have to set up machinery to overcome this. How will you do this?

You will give people jobs collecting the taxes and you will give them the power to do so and will pay them a living wage. What happens if the people your tax collectors visit offer them bribes to not collect the taxes, bribes that are five times the annual salary you are giving your people? Now you will have to enforce discipline on your tax collectors, so you will pay other people to be the police who watch the tax collectors and you will give them a living wage. But what if the corrupt people also bribe them? Who will you turn to now?

You see how it goes. You will soon find yourself building an enforcement mechanism that looks very much like the mechanisms of the old regime.

It is not as simple as you may have imagined to create the new world for which you are fighting. It is not just a matter of setting new policies. It is a matter of changing the existing culture. By definition, this does not happen easily or quickly. You cannot will it to happen. You must influence it to happen.

The people in power now are not doing things the way they are simply because they are evil. There is a system in place that rewards what they are doing. You must be very careful or that system will continue to reward your own people for doing things that way, too. And no, you cannot just eliminate everyone who may represent or succumb to that system. You will become the Khmer Rouge and fill your own killing fields. You cannot use the same tools to govern that you used to win the revolution. Force and summary justice will not build a new society. It will build a gulag. So what will you do?

Clearly you want to staff all your positions with "good" people who can set the example that you want others to live by. But how do you bring out this "good" in people? All of us are capable of either "good" or "bad" given the right circumstances.

You will need to personally be everywhere, setting the example. You will need to set the strongest example at the top of your own organization. At the first whiff of corruption you will have to remove that person from power, even if he is your closest friend. Especially if he is your closest friend. You will need to appear here and there, unexpectedly, complimenting examples of just and fair behavior, and chastising examples of laziness, indifference or greed. You will need to create the conditions that truly reward good acts and good people and slowly, slowly create a culture that embodies this behavior in its veins. Then you can build the institutions to support it and they will not become corrupt.

But what is a "good person"? Is it someone who agrees with you? That is a very dangerous definition of good. What makes you a good person or a bad person? We are into philosophy here. I am not a trained philosopher. But you and I are untrained philosophers. We think about these questions. We need to think about them.

I think that a good human being is someone who tolerates others who are different from himself and tries to treat them justly. He does not tolerate those who oppress others or who force others to be like themselves. Yes, tolerance for differences, intolerance of bullying and thuggery, fair treatment of all. That is what makes a good human being. This makes a person being capable of participating in and sustaining a just society. If this sounds too much like a "liberal", I am sorry. I believe it also possible and necessary to live this way as a radical and revolutionary.

Tolerance, I have concluded, is also a prerequisite for beneficial leadership. It is certainly not sufficient, but it is prerequisite. Not milquetoast tolerance of every harebrained or reactionary idea. Leaders must vigorously oppose these and energetically propose alternate, more compelling visions. But, at the same time, they must be tolerant of dissension or, with power in their grasp, they begin the tumble toward autocracy and brutality.

How do you make sure that you become a good human being? It takes work! It rarely just happens.

As a revolutionary leader, you must surround yourself with people of every age and every class and persuasion. And you must ask them about their views and actively discover how they differ from your views. You must seek to understand how they arrived at those views so you continually remain open to new ideas or new ways of reaching people with your ideas. It is a mistake to become afraid of new ideas, though we all do it. Pay attention to the ideas that jar you, that you resist. This is a test of newness. They may prove to be lousy or dangerous ideas, but it's healthy to examine your initial resistance to them before rejecting them.

You must also ask these diverse people you surround yourself with what they think of your ideas. What do they see as good and helpful? As unrealistic or harmful? You must become very comfortable with the viewpoint that rejecting your ideas is not the same as rejecting you or your leadership. Regardless of how much adulation your followers pour on you, your views are, of course, fallible. You need to always be searching for their fallibility, testing them for the days when there is no time to test them. You must convince people that you are interested in their true views, for they will be afraid to anger you, and you will only convince them of this if you sincerely appreciate what they tell you, however much it contradicts what you would like to hear. Don't use their opinions against them!

So where does that leave you as a revolutionary? I suggest, if you will permit the suggestions of an old comrade in arms who can barely raise those arms any longer, that it leaves you fighting a revolution against those who imprison, torture and murder people who disagree with or oppose them. And once you have won the people's freedom from this oppression, then you must influence the culture to live by a new set of values: compassion, tolerance, justice, respect for life. This will be a true revolution.

But you must recognize that there will be many people who see things differently from you and that you have also fought for their right to a differing reality. Yes, even in a religious revolution you must do this or you blaspheme against God who created all this diversity.

What a giant of a person you must be to do this. They did not fight! They did not risk everything! Still they have the right to differ!

But how do you influence a whole culture? How do you move a culture that has grown up on nepotism and bribery and corruption to shed these ways of behaving? How do you change the life long experience of subservience to masters? To not view these things as normal? You have your work cut out for you! And it cannot start after you have won the battle. It must start now and become a habit with you and those who surround you.

Everyday you will have opportunities to demonstrate the behaviors that you want to permeate the culture. A hundred eyes will watch you as you deal with people around you. Each time that you deal with others in ways consistent with the values of the revolution, but respectful of the differences they hold as human beings, you will sow a seed for the new culture. It sounds so easy, doesn't it? It's not. It's hard. Very hard.

You will be tired, exhausted, at your limit and you are expected to behave in such measured ways? It will be so much easier to fly off the handle and insist on your way! You have power. You have a gun in your hand. A commander's title. Whatever gives you power. It will be so easy to blow your stack! To make the other quiver and do what goddamn needs to be done!

Let me admit that it's effective to blow your top occasionally. It lets people know what's really important. But it will be so easy for you to behave this way every day. In every conversation. And then you will wonder why, after you have won the battle, you will lose the war of changing anything meaningfully. Because those around you will learn that it is still force which gets things done. And they will exchange one intimidating regime for another.

Let me suggest that you get down on your knees, or prostrate, or in a meditative posture everyday, in a gesture of great humility, and in your mind review the day and note every instance in which you did not behave as a model for what you want the culture to become. Turn your enormous will power inward for a brief period each day. Take pains to learn from every failure on your part. Humility is the only vaccination against for the abuse of power. And it is power that you are after.

What Makes a Good Human Being?

The task of becoming a true revolutionary is as hard as becoming a good human being!

Revolutionary Leaders

Maybe you are a revolutionary leader reading this. Maybe you are not a leader. Who cares? You are vital to the revolution.

If you are not the leader you will still be interested in this as you want to recognize and support leaders who will bring about the revolution, not blow it or betray it. If you are a leader you want to excel at your craft.

If you are a reader, you may have devoured classics on war and revolution. You may have read Sun Tzu, Mao, Clausewitz, Che, Paine, Fanon, and others. I am making my attempt to add to the readings that will interest you and help you.

Like all revolutionary leaders you are vain. You must be! You believe that you can change the world! I am even more vain! I believe that I can change the nature of revolution! In our mutual vanity, let us see what we can learn that may be of use!

A good question to begin with is what makes a revolutionary leader exceptional? All "successful" revolutionary leaders displace or alter the power structure they resolved to overthrow. The exceptional leader replaces it with a more just and competent regime. That is the outcome. But what qualities permit the exceptional leader to do this?

I have thought about this a long time and have distilled these qualities down to seven pairs or sets of characteristics. I cannot swear to you they are the best distillation possible. But I can assure you they are each important, so important that you cannot afford to be seriously deficient in any one of them.

The qualities in these sets are juxtaposed, one against another, and form a creative tension. You could say that they are in dynamic balance. These sets are:

Reality & Vision

Patience & Decisiveness

Confidence & Humility

Compassion & Pragmatism

Learning & Teaching

Persistence & Flexibility

Self-Reliance and Self-Devolution

You know that I am going to expound on each of these. That is my self-appointed job: to give you advice whether or not you have asked me for it. So pay attention and see what you can learn.

Reality & Vision

The non-leader swims in a murky sense of life. He does not form a crystal sharp understanding of what exists and how it got here. Nor does he form an equally clear picture of a possible future for which it is worth fighting, and even dying.

The strong leader sees what is. He does not fool himself. He does not imagine the power structure is weaker than it is, that the army will desert at his first urging, that foreign powers will rush to his aid when their own self-interest does not demand it. He sees reality. It is the ability to see and describe reality for what it is that both motivates him and tempers him.

The leader also sees what the future may become. His vision is brilliantly clear to himself. Sometimes he is blessed with the ability to make it equally vivid to others through the passion and images of his speech. It is not a utopian vision. Utopian visions fail and profoundly disappoint. It is not so lofty as to be unachievable, but it is sufficiently lofty to be worth striving for. It is a vision fully informed by the living aspirations of the people he serves, whom he allows to influence and reshape ideological visions he has brought to them.

The gap between reality and this vision represents the political, cultural, economic and spiritual journey which must occur. It gives rise to the strategy that the leader will employ to make the journey. This is where all your other reading comes in handy, to help you understand the structure of resistance to revolutionary change. It will be your task to use that understanding to devise ways your people can cross the chasm to a better reality.

Patience & Decisiveness

The shrewd leader knows when to still his need for action, when to honor the value of patience. The ability to wait until the right moment to act is worth three divisions of men, or the control of several media outlets.

Patience is the great balance to individual will. It acknowledges that we cannot force ourselves on the universe. We can only pay attention to moments and places of opportunity and exploit them with all the energy and knowledge we bring to the event. Without patience, the leader takes the wrong risks and then relies on the fickle ally, luck. Without patience the leader inflicts or incurs excessive suffering, violating the proportionality of means and ends.

The competent leader equally knows the moment for action and commits his resources decisively. He knows full well the odds and the risks. He knows how much information he does not have and cannot obtain that would support or refute his decision. He understands the accountability he bears for his decisions and the consequences of his judgment should it be wrong. Knowing all this, he nevertheless acts with the energy and conviction needed to marshal the full strength and spirit of those who follow him into action. He does not squirm and hedge and cause others to doubt if this is the moment to risk their lives and fortunes.

These two qualities, patience and decisiveness, must go hand in hand as opposite as they may seem. The effective leader does not lean too far in either direction, and treats a tendency to do so as a sign that he is becoming too passive or too cocky. He looks for opportunities to restore the balance, keeping his people informed about his reasoning so they do not interpret his actions as vacillation and become dispirited.

Confidence & Humility

The revolutionary leader draws strength from a deep and personal well. If he is successful, or even unsuccessful but legendary, historians will write tomes seeking to explain him to the world. But it is unlikely that anyone will fully understand the source of his strength. When the leader possesses this inner strength, his self-confidence permits him to surround himself with strong men and women who will amplify his vision and energy. He does not need the yes-men and lackeys who surround weaker leaders.

From this same well of self-confidence comes the understanding that no man is perfect. If he is to serve his people who have placed so much of their hopes in his ability to use power well, he must do what he humanly can do to understand his own weaknesses and have those around him compensate for these with his blessing. This is the humility that breeds reverence for a leader. Only in the face of this humility can reverence safely be bestowed.

Compassion & Pragmatism

Except for a handful of saints, leaders are driven in part by concern for the people they serve and in part by a desire for admiration or power. Like a recipe needing both sugar and salt, this is not a problem if mixed in appropriate proportions. A great revolutionary leader will always have a large proportion of compassion in that mix.

This will not be a theoretical compassion for "the people" but a gut level compassion for this child and that woman and this man, for that family and this village and that minority. If he begins to lose that visceral connection, he moves out among the people again and reconnects to what the revolution is about. He does not let himself become removed from the people he serves. You cannot believe how easy it is to become removed, while deluding yourself that you know the people! It takes a conscious act, and a habit of getting out from your headquarters and away from your retinue to avoid this.

The compassion of the leader is not sweet and sappy and full of wishful thoughts. It is pragmatic and is expressed in the most down-to-earth, common sense acts of timely help to people who need it. There are times when you may hear the leader let loose a blast aimed at those around him who are being complacent about others' suffering. There are times that he will, as they say in my adopted country, kick ass to see that relief supplies are gotten to those in distress, regardless of the obstacles. Real help, not slogans is what the effective leader will deliver.

Learning & Teaching

The prerequisite to learning is curiosity. Why did other revolutions succeed or fail? Is the conventional wisdom about these true, or too shallow an understanding? Why are downtrodden people reluctant to turn against an oppressive regime? What do they fear more than the regime? Why did I behave the way I did in the revolutionary council meeting today? Was the reason I gave myself the whole story, or not? Curiosity, curiosity, curiosity. It marks the leader who can continue to grow throughout his or her life.

Once curiosity is present, then methods of learning become relevant. Maybe some leaders learn by reading historic, economic or sociological books, but not you. In such a case you may develop a defensive scorn for those who read too much. This is an unhealthy and dangerous reaction for a revolutionary. Recognize that people learn in different ways. Maybe for you it would be more productive to have discussions with those who enjoy reading about the events and lives they are studying. You may be someone who learns by hearing. Or, maybe you learn better by seeing and touching and it is better for others to demonstrate subjects to you using diagrams, artifacts, site inspections and other direct means. The essential factor is to honor learning. Men who acquire great power and have little desire or capacity to learn are the most dangerous on earth. Learn all the time. Learn from your generals, from your aide-de-camp, from your cook, from your enemy. Life is one great school.

As you learn, you must teach. Not ponderous teaching. Not windbag teaching. Not four-hour revolutionary harangues. I never stopped cursing how this became the fashion of revolutionary leaders in my lifetime! Talk, talk, talk. People learn to stand at attention and appear to be listening, while their minds are blank or they are entertaining themselves with thoughts of a picnic on a riverbank!

These harangues are a dangerous practice as the leader comes to believe that all truth emanates from him, that he is central and indispensable. This should be the last concept a revolutionary leader adopts of his role! He is first and foremost a servant of the people. Yes, there is some prophet thrown in! But there is a fine line between seeing oneself as the prophet and the god!

Think, instead, how real learning occurs. Learning occurs most powerfully by example. If growing up, I see a man taking care of his children and family, I learn what it is to be a man. If I grow up seeing men sitting around the street gambling their money on cockfights while their children go hungry, I learn the wrong way to be a man.

As a revolutionary leader, people watch your actions, your deeds, what you reward, what you punish, how you spend your time, what you spend money on, how you treat people. These are the things they learn from. Not four-hour speeches.

The revolutionary leader teaches by being aware of himself as an example in everything he decides or does. He teaches by seeing the opportunities in each day to focus the attention of those around him on what is important and right. He teaches by seeing the opportunities to shine a light on old ways of thinking. He does this not to humiliate those around him, but to help them see how they still carry the old ways within them, and how they can learn to think and behave in new ways.

Persistence & Flexibility

I think of each pair of characteristics as a brace of oxen. They pull together to get the job done. The next brace of characteristics of the outstanding revolutionary leader begin with discipline – self-discipline. This is difficult, at least for me. It may be one of the reasons I didn't rise to a leadership role. Who knows? It's difficult to see oneself clearly.

No leader needs to be perfectly self-disciplined. The few I have seen who came close to being perfect, also came close to being inhuman, to the detriment of those around them. Perfection is both unnecessary and undesirable.

But a great leader has a large degree of self-discipline. He is a professional and behaves like one. He knows that his people count on him to be visible, to show up where he is needed and to be consistent in what others can expect of him (with a few surprises to keep them on their toes). He masters himself sufficiently to do these things despite the times he does not feel up to doing so or craves to be elsewhere.

The greatest discipline is that of persistence. When others lose heart and are on the verge of giving up, the leader finds it within himself to keep going and to rally his comrades. When the very tide washes against them, when the chances of success seem bleak, the leader holds the belief that their cause will prevail, that they will overcome the direst predictions and realize the just fruits of their awesome labor. Though he has repeatedly reached a certain point and been pushed back again year after year, the next year he will try a new strategy to win the ground again, and then some! He does not forget the goal, he does not get distracted from it by vendettas or fatigue. He persists when it seems the gods of justice themselves have given up.

The balance to this unquenchable persistence is flexibility. Years of being steadfast and unwavering do not rob the leader of the capacity to be flexible when the moment for flexibility arrives. His very steadfastness earns him the right to display flexibility when he judges this will best serve the cause, without others interpreting flexibility as selling out or betrayal. Though all around him doubt the enemy can ever be trusted, he persists in looking for the face saving opportunity to allow the enemy a chance to negotiate. Though he has described and defined the enemy for decades, he recognizes the moment when the interests of both sides coincide and negotiation is possible.

By retaining this flexibility of mind and attitude and strategy, he does not waste a lifetime's work. Instead, he realizes the best that can be realized for his people. Like a fighter who goes fifteen rounds, he has not knocked out his opponent, but he nevertheless can win by a judgment. This is the best he was able to do, and victory comes in different ways.

Self-Reliance and Self-Devolution

To win the war, the leader has required enormous depths of self-reliance. While he has sought and welcomed the views and concerns and wisdom of others, he has relied on his instincts and judgments and resolution to cross all the deepest rivers.

Now the war has been won. Does he take this self-reliance and build his administration on it? Does he do more of what made the revolution successful? It would seem to be the right thing to do, but hear me my revolutionary leader, it is the worst thing you can do.

In victory lies your greatest danger. The people will adulate you. They will do what you want. They will pressure you to build institutions of government around your own person. You will seem to be the only glue that can hold the revolution and all its factions together. You will succumb to these forces and become the last thing you should become.

Yes, you need to continue to provide leadership for a period. But it shall be what I call the leadership of self-devolution. I confess I have made up this word as I do not know another that captures the concept well enough. With every act you take, every policy decision you make, every institution you design you must ask "Does this lead the country away from reliance on me?" and only proceed if the answer is "yes".

If you are making decisions that keep the country reliant on you, you are setting the country up for its next revolution or civil war. Even if you were to use your power only for the good of your people, the fact that you retained power for twenty years will cause them to remain ignorant of how to conduct transitions. And the chances are not very good that you would continue to use power well over such a long period of time. I invite you, please, to look at the record of your fellow revolutionaries in the last century and see for yourself.

Though you will cause your countrymen great anxiety, you must program your own transition out of power almost from the beginning. To do this you must hold two visions: a personal and a national, because it is more powerful to work towards a positive vision than to work away from a negative one.

The first vision is personal. You must see yourself truly free of the responsibilities and perks of the burden of power. You must see yourself clearly retired in your country estate, or your modest village home, with a whole different set of things around you that give life meaning and joy: your children and grandchildren, your writing projects, gardening, painting or music, good friends, charities to which you are devoting your name and energy –anything but the political.

The second vision is for your country. You must see clearly in your mind's eye an orderly succession process. Only this will provide the stability your country needs now. You must be prepared to see your successors stumble in their efforts and see yourself sitting back, clucking over errors, but not riding in to save them. You are always available if they seek advice, but you never use up your welcome with presumptuous advice that undermines their self-respect and confidence.

So, there it is! The team of oxen that will pull your revolution to a true victory! Yes, I am being preachy! Maybe I sound like a pain in the ass old man! But, if your cause is important enough to foment revolution, it is important enough for you to know your strengths and weaknesses as one of its leaders. No wriggling off the hook! Assess yourself as you would assess the quality of troops at your disposal. Face yourself with the determination and courage with which you face the enemy. Then develop a plan of attack and stick to the plan.

Here's what to do. Place these qualities in order, from your strongest to your weakest. This will help you clarify and play to your strengths. Then begin working to improve your weaknesses, just as a professional athlete would do who takes his or her career seriously. Surely, you must take your career as seriously as an athlete! So much more is at stake.

I would suggest that officer cadres hold each other accountable for doing this. The character of the leadership team determines the character of the revolution. In the name of all the people who have died and who will die for the revolution, make it a worthwhile character!

Revolutionary Followers

Now it is time to talk to you, the follower of this leader to whom I have been speaking.

You are preoccupied to some degree with the business of living your life. And so you should be. You have children to feed or a girlfriend to keep happy. You have old parents who need support or crops that need to be harvested. You have so little margin between you and catastrophe. You have aspirations to improve your life, even a little bit. Yet the revolution is now and is demanding your energy now.

You have great faith in your leader. He is counting on you. You do not want to let him down. You would sooner let your mother or father down. He has become like a father. He has taught you so much. He believes in you and what you can do. He offers you hope for a better life for your children. He offers you dignity and freedom from the humiliation the repressive regime heaps on you. You agree to do things you would rather not do, or you did not believe that you could do or would do, as you do not want to let him down. You and your comrades are part of what makes him great, as you are willing to follow him and accomplish impossible things in his name.

You look to him as you would to a savior, almost as you would to a god. But, you see that he is vulnerable. He can become sullen and depressed. He can exhaust himself. He can have tantrums. He can get sick and drag himself through his duties. His wife can abandon him or he can be unfaithful to her. He can drink too much or he can never allow himself to drink and unwind.

Your god – I'm sorry – your leader, is invaluable to your cause. He is a rallying point. He embodies all the hopes you did not dare to hope without him. He touches people who consider themselves natural enemies and brings them together against their common enemy. He captures the imagination and has people secretly hoping for his success who would not dare to publicly admit it. He shames powerful people into quiet alliances with him as they see the sacrifices he is willing to make. They contribute some of their fortune or reputation because he is contributing his life. They trust him and he must continue to deserve their trust, or their support will collapse like a house of cards when a door is slammed in anger. How do you help him hold himself together when he is under so much pressure from inside himself and from outside?

Well, you had better start by knocking off this "god" bullshit. I know it was my word, not yours, but if you'd admit it, my word comes closer to how you feel about him than your words. So you're setting him up for failure. He's not a god. He never will be. So he doesn't need worshipers around him. He needs comrades. He needs friends, whether or not he'll allow himself to have any. He needs people who don't expect more of him than is realistic and don't tell him that he's better than he actually is.

Yes, he needs loyalty. But loyalty to both him and the truth. Don't sacrifice one for the other. It's not loyalty to let him believe what he wants to believe. It's loyalty to look him in the eye and tell him what you see even if you infuriate him. It's the only way you will help him avoid catching the "king's sickness." You know, the sickness in which he deludes himself into thinking that everything he thinks is true. Even when he thinks he is well dressed, though he is buck-naked.

He may reprove you up and down and tear strips off your pride if you tell him the truth, but he will value you as someone he can always come to when he needs another point of view. Actually, it's better if you don't let him bawl you out too much as that will become a bad habit on his part. It will intimidate the others around him. He won't get the best out of them. Take him up on this, too. Tell him nothing gives him the right to treat people that way. Tell him to save his anger for when the people's business warrants it. Not when he wants to bully someone into accepting his way of doing things. If he wants a true revolution, stop acting like a fucking king!

And you'd better watch your own contribution to his distemper! There's a lot of ways that you can do this. You're not responsible for his emotional state, but you are responsible for providing him good enough support that his temper doesn't unnecessarily fray.

Now let me tell you something that will sound very strange. This man needs to take vacations. Who ever heard of a revolutionary taking a vacation? That's a bourgeois concept if there ever was one! Nevertheless, he needs vacations, even mini-vacations. They can be as simple as dragging him out of his tent down to the river and throwing him in the water for a change of pace! Or hand him a fishing pole! Or get him incognito and arrange for him to go to a football game or a religious celebration or a museum of antiquities. Something to break up the seriousness with which he wakes up and goes to sleep everyday.

Keep him in contact with as many people as security allows. Do not permit him to become isolated from the people in whose name he acts. Do not let him become a theoretical champion of "the people" while he becomes bad tempered and abuses the real people who work for him.

Recognize that you'd follow him to the end of the earth, but be clear that you will not jump off it for him. Or allow him to fall off it, at least not without a damn good rescue effort.

This business of revolution is harder than anyone thinks. On the one hand, it does give everyone concerned meaning to their life. It's a lucky person who has a strong sense of meaning about his or her life. Most people just get through the week and year relying on time and biology to keep them moving forward. Someone who has found meaning through art or scientific discovery or compassionate service to others, feels ten times more alive. Only a great love can rival this feeling. Sometimes we have periods of life in which we have this experience and later we look back on these times as golden periods. Those lucky enough to be engaged in revolutionary action, in a whole new beginning for their people, experience life this way.

On the other hand, the price you pay is steep. Very steep. The leaders are under enormous pressure. Every day they must make decisions that will have larger consequences than the decisions that most people make in a lifetime. Their decisions will result in whether people are fed or go hungry, whether people will live or die, whether the government will retaliate massively or not, whether the revolution will secure allies or remain isolated, become corrupted or stay pure.

Like you, the leaders often bear enormous personal hardship. They are unavailable to their young children who need them, they are watching their brother rot in a jail while unable to free him, they cannot visit their home or the homes of their friends that are under surveillance, their parents have been ostracized for their son's activities and live out their final years in gloomy isolation.

Their health, like yours, is neglected. They cannot or will not get the medical attention they need. It is not available or not safe. They often move about to stay ahead of the informers and spies and have no place to rest. Warmth and dry clothes are luxuries they cannot count on. The water may be bad. Injuries and wounds must be borne as they go through their daily actions. There is no time for rest and proper healing. Of course, this is not so different from the experience of the people for whom they are fighting.

These hardships must be mitigated within your limited capacity to do so. Don't underestimate the effect even minor medical attention can have. When an itinerant doctor eased the bunions on Abraham Lincoln's feet, it made a remarkable difference to his outlook which always bordered on the depressed during a long, bloody war and a string of family tragedies. Che suffered horribly when he could not get access to his asthma medication.

It takes a sunny disposition to bear hardships with grace. Revolutionary leaders are not often born with such dispositions. If they were, they may not have developed the critical mass of outrage to start a revolution. So they often walk a fine line between purposeful action and depression. If they succumb to the depression the revolution can go for months without clear direction and then be yanked into fitful action. If they can't stand the depression, the leader will keep it at bay with frenetic activity, lashing out unproductively and sometimes cruelly in many directions. None of this serves the cause well.

So do not underestimate your role in softening these hardships. Do not let the gruff bear always isolate himself. Cajole him into the comfort of a game of cards with comrades. Pull him out of his tent when the balladeer is singing around the fire. If there's a biologist in your midst, have him give field classes on the awesome complexity of life so everyone's mind, including the leader's, stays fresh and stimulated.

My point is that as much as life is a battle, it must also remain a celebration. If life deteriorates into only a battle, then all interactions will be viewed as a battle. This will justify any type of action against others and your revolution will be lost. At its core, a successful revolution must honor life and revel in life and be fighting the forces that make life unnecessarily grim. Therefore, the revolution itself must not become grim though the forces pulling its leaders in this direction are always enormous.

While you are fighting the revolution you, as one of the few who are close to your leaders, must also tend to the internal revolution. You are brave, you are good hearted. Your leaders trust you. Use that trust to make them do things that will keep them behaving as good human beings. There is great wisdom in the relaxation of ordinary folk. Genius and ambition often rejects this. But if you put the power of life and death in their hands, it is very dangerous for them to lose touch with the simple acts that help people live together. Keep an element of simple joys in the revolutionary diet. Don't wait for permission to do this. It will never come. Just do it, using your love for the leader to persuade his participation.

I haven't told a story in so long. It is time for a story.

Celebration

It was an agonizing day for Ahmed. He wished the day had never come. He had finished prayers and cleaning his rifle as he did every morning. While drinking his bitter field coffee, the messenger came.

"My leader. We have captured him."

Ahmed did not need to ask who they had captured. It was his cousin, Mustafa.

"Where did you find him?"

"He was hiding in a cave, halfway to their compound."

"Where is he now?"

"We are bringing him back here. The party will arrive this afternoon, my leader."

"You have done well," Ahmed said, masking his agony from the messenger. "Go and refresh yourself."

Mustafa had been Ahmed's favorite. They grew up together like brothers. He was as brave as any of the resistance fighters. On several occasions he had risked his life to save comrades and everyone knew of his bravery. This should never have happened. But it did. And now the leader had to lead, showing no favorites.

Mustafa had given signs of discontent for several weeks. When Ahmed talked with him, Mustafa did not disguise his confusion. He was no longer sure they were doing the right thing. Perhaps they should have accepted the compromise the enemy had offered. The killing had gone on so long. They were all so tired.

Ahmed had ordered Mustafa to rest for several days, hoping this would restore his attitude. He had wanted to give him home leave, but it was too dangerous. All of their houses were under surveillance and several safe houses had been raided in the last month.

On the third day of his base leave, Mustafa disappeared from camp. The alarm was raised and the general area was scoured. There was no trace of him. Ahmed knew the signs. Something had snapped in Mustafa and he was preparing to make his own truce with the enemy. But Ahmed knew the price the enemy extracted for this and he could not allow the deal to be made.

He ordered a search party. They were to head in the direction of the enemy's main compound, three days walk to the south. He gave them horses and his best tracker.

On the third day they found Mustafa. He did not try to fight them. He sat and cried for a while. Then rose and began walking back with them.

He would be here soon, Ahmed thought. We have had four desertions towards the enemy lines under my command. Three I ordered shot. The fourth was a boy of thirteen, so it was understood when I gave him another chance. I cannot give Mustafa another chance.

Ahmed was interrupted in his thoughts.

"My leader. We wish to speak with you." Three of his most trusted lieutenants were at the entrance to his tent.

"Come in and speak," Ahmed replied, not showing that he was startled out of his reverie.

"I will speak for the group," said Khalil, the eldest. "We have discussed the matter and concluded it is not proper that you should have to sit in judgment of your cousin. The burden is too great on you to decide between your loyalty to your family and your loyalty to the resistance. We will sit in judgment of Mustafa. We will weigh his transgressions against his contributions and decide his punishment."

Ahmed sat in silence for a moment, then replied. "You are faithful followers and I must thank you for your concern. But it is my responsibility to bear the burden of leadership and pass this judgment. I cannot shirk my responsibility." His voice carried the weight of a great sadness covered with a fragile skin of courage and duty.

Khalil nodded in understanding and replied. "We greatly admire your willingness to carry the burden of leadership though it comes close to breaking the back of its carrier. But, in this instance, we are not here to ask your indulgence for our request. We are exercising our responsibility as your *senior commanders to relieve you of this burden, without shame to you. We will hear Mustafa's case and pass judgment on him."*

For a moment a hard streak flashed through Ahmed's body and mind. The leader's instinctive response to a threat to his leadership activated. He could hear in his mind the great butting of rams' horns as they fought for dominance. First Mustafa and now this!

Then, just as suddenly, another streak washed through his body. A streak of relief and gratitude. Someone was sharing the great burden of leadership with him. In this case, the unbearable burden.

Ahmed looked at Khalil. "You are wise in your resolve. I will follow your counsel."

"We have one more decision to convey to you. Tomorrow, after evening prayer, after the decision on what to do with Mustafa has been made and executed, we will have a gathering. It will be a gathering with music and dancing and contests. As we do not yet know our judgment, we do not know if the gathering will be a celebration or a mourning. It is immaterial. We all need to shake from our hearts the burden that has been placed there. Our gathering will help us do this."

On the second night after this conversation, the hills echoed with the beating of goatskin drums. If you had been in the right place to observe, you would have seen scores of men wildly circling the small fires, casting enormous shadows on the mountain walls. Preparations had been made to break camp and move before dawn, as the fires and noise would surely give away their location. But that night, there was a great surge of energy emanating from the chanting, whirling men. A great release of the tensions of months of resistance.

Ahmed could be seen whirling as fast and hard as any of the dancers. He picked up other men and spun them on his shoulders. They, in turn, grabbed him by the wrists and spun him off the ground like an airplane. They linked arms and stomped left around the fire, then right around the fire. Sweat poured from their foreheads and left zigzag trails down their dust covered faces. The fires danced in their eyes as they danced in its warmth.

Ahmed's voice could be picked out from the waves of chanting. At times it came from deep within his chest. At other times it wailed from the top of his throat. Always, his voice was full and urgent, calling to an unseen listener, enticing them to listen with its strength and beauty and earnestness. He sang till his voice was a whisper and the night was almost done.

Before dawn broke, if you were an observer, you would wonder, had this been a mourning or a celebration?

Preparing to Govern

Now I am going to talk to you about preparing to govern. You might think that I'm mad raising this subject now. You probably control a small fraction of the country or enjoy the support of a small minority of the population. You're sure that your attention must remain on organizing the countryside and fighting the current battles. I'm not so sure, not so sure at all. Let me tell you why.

It seems tough leading a revolution and it is tough. But wait and see. It is not as tough as governing. You are probably snorting when you hear me say that. It sounds like such a stupid statement. When you govern you will be rich with resources. Now you are dirt poor. What could be tougher?

Here's the catch. All cultures are complex. Cultures that are relatively advanced economically and technologically are incredibly complex. The people who live in them lose all sense as to how complex they are. Simple acts of buying food from a supermarket in an urban area require so much underlying infrastructure that you would be staggered once you put it all together. We routinely underestimate by a factor of ten what it takes to keep our level of civilization operating.

Living in the hills or hiding on the margins of this civilization can make its mechanisms seem deceptively simpler than they are. But when you are responsible for governing a system that requires millions of people to get their food and clothing and housing and transportation provided through this complex system you need to appreciate what is involved.

All too often revolutionaries devote every ounce of energy to surviving and to winning their revolution and indoctrinating recruits and the populace in the tenets of the revolution. Then one day they wake up and they are in power. What do they do now? It seems simple. They stay true to their principles. They get rid of everybody who ran the old regime. They install their own faithful, the people who won the revolution. How often does this work? How much more often do the wheels of production soon grind to a halt? After a couple of years the people find themselves, unbelievably, with even less food and clothing and jobs than they had before. How did this happen? The victorious revolutionaries got rid of the people who understood the incredible complexity of the economy.

Or the opposite happens. The revolutionaries win. Perhaps they struck a deal at the end to remove the last organized opposition to their efforts. They move into power and, recognizing their own lack of experience with governing, they retain technocrats from the old regime to stabilize the situation. Nothing changes. There is no greater justice, no improved distribution of wealth, no less corrupt policing. The people grow cynical at having once again been betrayed.

The alternative to these scenarios is preparing to govern before one has earned the power to govern. This is an important idea for many reasons. The first, which you will appreciate, is that it reinforces the vision that one day you will be governing. I have said this to you before. Vision is powerful. It precedes a new reality.

Another reason is that preparing to govern challenges you and your followers to grow. Growth will be necessary to use power well when you have at last wrested it from those who are misusing it. Because you are on the side of the righteous does not mean you will be on the side of the competent when your time comes. I am sorry, but this is a reality you are better off facing now.

You need to work hard to develop skills that may not be natural to you. In doing this you will establish dialogues with people who are involved in these things and understand them well. You may even find that, in the process of preparing yourself to govern, you build the coalitions to do so without a revolutionary victory. Perhaps enough will change that it will become meaningful to share power rather than continuing to fight to wrest it away. Your options increase. Yes, there is the danger that you will become co-opted by the system. Revolution is full of danger and that has not stopped you from taking its risks.

There is another important benefit to preparation. When you yourself wrestle with the complexity of governing you become less arrogant about those who came before you. When you are less arrogant you will not be as scathing in your judgment of others and are less likely to be excessively punitive towards them. It is better that you become a nation builder than a judge and executioner.

A final and perhaps the most important benefit is that when you are well prepared to govern you will feel more secure. This allows you to surround yourself with competent people without feeling threatened by them. It allows you to tolerate mistakes, your own and others, without becoming paranoid about counterrevolutionary activity. It helps you make more right than wrong decisions and to behave more calmly when wrong decisions have to be righted.

If you owe it to the people to fight for them, you owe it to the people to prepare yourself and your supporters for governing. How do you do so? Let your imagination guide you. There are a hundred ways. The important thing is that you do it. You probably already are doing some of them because you understand the need. Do more. It is never enough.

Perhaps, for example, you assign a team to prepare briefings on each of the key subsystems that keep the current society running. You request a sophisticated description of how it functions, the many levels of formal and informal bodies that contribute to it and the processes they use. You ask your teams to make recommendations about how to simplify and improve the subsystems based on the values that guide the revolution. What are the options for making each subsystem more fair, responsive and honest, while keeping it at least as productive as it has been to date? If you are going to do away with the system altogether, how will the legitimate functions it serves are taken care of? By doing this you develop pools of knowledge and expertise from which you can draw when the time comes.

Perhaps you recruit learned men and women to educate you and your team. Yes, to put you through school and help you learn what you don't even know that you don't know. I don't mean political indoctrination, though this may be important for purposes of movement identity. I mean governance training. So you know enough about each area to ask the right questions, to appoint the right administrators, to support good processes that involve the people in effective decision-making.

Perhaps like many revolutionary groups you set up a shadow government, but you take it further. You practice running the country every day. You think about the situations the radio is reporting and what you know about them. You learn what other information you would need to understand them. You test out what changes you would make in conformance with your revolutionary principles. You work out the likely impact of those changes and evaluate your options if the impact is not what you wanted it to be.

However you do this, you must come to understand how the major sub-systems work, as flawed and unjust as they may seem. You can only successfully reorganize them if you understand their complexity.

Perhaps the judicial system stinks. So you bypass it entirely and set up revolutionary courts. If those courts lack safeguards against becoming as unjust to ethnic groups as the current legal system, they will discredit the revolution. But who has done the groundwork to ensure the revolutionary legal system will work, that it will avoid the pitfalls that made the old system a cesspool? You think you can establish the new system by decree? In that case, you are already substituting one authoritarian regime for another. Study, discussion, briefing, education, planning, testing and fine-tuning are all needed to make the system work when it is show time.

Finance and economics are even trickier. You have many enemies who would like to see you fail in this sphere so they can take back control. It is a complicated sphere. Maybe the financial systems are purposefully made complex by the greedy who don't want people to be able to understand the ways in which they are being cheated.

But there are some absolute basics that must be understood. People must retain confidence in the monetary system so they will use it to acquire or provide needed goods and services. To do this there must be enough money in circulation to facilitate the exchange of these goods and services. At the same time, the currency must hold its value so that people can make orderly predictions about their futures. You must learn enough so that your decisions support these fundamentals.

Some may say that this is not revolutionary thinking, but status quo thinking posing as revolutionary advice. Perhaps so. But I say to you, take the time to understand the existing system before acting to dismantle it. There may be pieces that must be saved at least for an interim period, if not as integral parts of any new system. Find out as much of this as you can before you act, not afterwards. If you fail to understand the complexity of the system, you will bring about more, not less misery when you are in power. And you may learn, all too quickly, that people will then value order and the price of bread before revolutionary ideals. They will turn away from you and all that you have dedicated your life to.

If you do not prepare yourself to govern you may gather as much power as Chairman Mao and then make mistakes as stupid as the ones he made in the Great Leap Forward. It is a great shame, because there was a time when Mao took learning seriously and did what he could to educate himself. Then he rejected learning and became convinced of his own omniscience. Before the Great Leap Forward, this terribly conceived initiative, China could largely feed herself. Afterwards, tens of millions starved to death. How did this occur? Through Chairman Mao's ignorance combined with his nearly total power. He confused revolutionary will with competence. So he ordered everyone to set up smelting furnaces in their villages to outstrip England's steel production capacity while he amalgamated their farms into huge, factory-like collectives. He did not take seriously the need to understand the enormous complexity of transforming an agrarian economy to an industrial economy.

With what result? You know the outcome! Millions of people who should have been planting and tending their fields were diverted to industrial projects, including building and running backyard smelting furnaces, never mind the quality of their output. And from where were they to get the ore to produce steel? Never mind. This was the revolution! They took their cooking and serving pots and melted them down to ingots! The result? Millions of homes stripped of functional utensils and left instead with inferior grade steel ingots to demonstrate the power of the people's revolution to produce steel! And the larger result? Famine from years of neglecting their crops and massive disruption to their working farms.

We come back to a repeating point. Your intention and your job are to make people's lives better, not worse. The fact that you are committed to making their lives better does not mean that you will do so. You must learn how to make their lives better. To do that you must learn what supports their lives at their current levels of existence as well as what holds them back. Then you can use the vitality of the revolution to experiment with ways to make these things better.

You'd better have whole classes of your followers learning each of the key disciplines. A few at the top are not enough. They will become elites. Besides, you are revolutionaries. Who will live and who will die is not yet known. Who will stay true and who will give up or betray is not yet certain. Who will prove trustworthy with power and who will distort its use is yet to be revealed.

You cannot wait. You are readying yourself all at once for the battle you must win this morning and the one you must win next year or a decade from now. You are leading and you are preparing to lead, you are governing what is yours to govern and you are preparing yourself to govern that over which you intend to exert stewardship.

So clean your rifle and then go to class. You must become that which you expect the world to become. Work on it today, as today is all you have with certainty.

Good King Alfred

It's time for me to tell you another story. The nights are long and people need stories to keep them entertained. They remember a good story. They tell it to others. They pass it on to their children.

This time I will tell you a "real" story. A his-story. It is about King Alfred, the only king of England ever to be called "The Great" and the only one to deserve it. But he was also called Good King Alfred and he was also the only one to deserve that title. Imagine, in over a thousand years of kings and queens, the only one to be called both good and great. This must be a life worth examining.

Of course, it is strange in a book on revolution to be extolling the virtues of a king. It would seem that I have crossed over to the side of entrenched power. But you will soon see that this is not at all the case. Like you, Alfred hid out in the swamps and forests to evade the army that was sent to exterminate him. Like you, he had to depend on the direct support of the people to supply him and to keep his whereabouts secret. But how did all this occur, that a king was in the swamp being hunted? And what is it that made him good and great?

You must imagine a very young man of twenty-two, recently and unexpectedly ascended to the throne of his ancient kingdom, more than a thousand years ago. He was the youngest of five brothers, and suffered, like Che, from a chronic painful disease. It was wildly unlikely that he would ever lead his people. But, with the uncertainty that accompanies all of life, his four elder brothers and their father died within a few years of each other, thrusting Alfred into his fateful role.

He was well taught by his father, King Aethelwulf. As you know all too well, those with power fight to get more of it, putting their insatiable desires over the needs of their people. Alfred's father, with foresight and wisdom, constructed careful formulas for the distribution of his property and titles among his sons to minimize this scourge of human existence. When his eldest son died he again carefully distributed power and property between his remaining sons before embarking on a journey to what were then the

Gallic and Frankish Kingdoms and Rome. He took his youngest son, Alfred, with him, exposing him to cultures more advanced than his own, sowing the seeds of Alfred's vision for what his own land could become.

While they traveled, the next oldest son, Aethelbald, plotted to take his father's throne. When the King returned from his travels with Alfred, rather than plunge his kingdom into the miseries of civil war, with great forbearance he again negotiated an arrangement that all the parties could live with

Just as well, for they could hardly afford to drain their energies in internal warfare. Invaders from across the North Sea, the Vikings, were about to change their lives forever. The Norsemen began sending their young men on raiding parties to the British Isles. At first these were just summer excursions, though deadly enough. The raiders, young, fierce, out to prove themselves and to begin making their fortunes, plundered and killed as they made their forays inland from the east coast of the islands. Their targets proved poorly organized and easy to take.

Encouraged by the ease of the pickings, they soon sent a force of army strength. As they wreaked their havoc, the King of Mercia, the neighbor to the North of Wessex, asked for Aethelwulf's help. He rode to Mercia with Alfred by his side where early on he learned the fearsome martial strength of these Vikings.

The battles were indecisive and the Vikings came and went at their pleasure as the Saxons made their best efforts to repulse them from Mercia and Wessex. In other parts of England, the Vikings were gaining more of a foothold. Life was lived with the ominous prospect of Viking domination never far from the mind. The people of England were in grave danger of losing their independence, their land, their Anglo-Saxon culture, their Christian religion and their English language to this more effective force. It was during this crucial period that Alfred's father and older brothers died.

Alfred could not have become King at a worse moment. A clear shift was occurring. A second Viking army had landed, prepared to stay in England for years, intent on conquest. England was not yet a united country, but a collection of independent kingdoms. The original Viking army had already conquered or wrested tribute from most of these kingdoms, leaving themselves free to concentrate on the remaining holdouts. They had captured and publicly torn apart from limb to limb one of the other kings, a calculated act designed to instill dread in anyone who might attempt to resist them.

So here we have a lad of twenty two with the responsibility for the survival of his country and culture in his hands, bereaved of all the familial support with which he had grown up, afflicted by a mysterious disease that periodically incapacitated him with excruciating pain, faced with a brutal foe, to which several of his neighboring kings had already fallen, who threatened to brutally dismember any king who dared resist them and failed. Alfred's men were exhausted and they faced a new, fresh army.

As if the external challenge was not enough, the sons of one of his brothers, Aethlred, were contesting Alfred's right to rule parts of the kingdom to which they felt entitled. He urgently needed around him men who would fight, men who would work the land and men who would keep what was left of the culture together. He needed to find ways to support them with food, drink, clothing, shelter, weapons and rewards. He needed to keep their morale sufficient to the task, transform their doubts into confidence and stem the contagion of despair or panic. You will recognize these elements and Alfred's desperate need to cope with them. You will not be surprised to learn that he had great, if silent misgivings about his ability to lead in these trying circumstances.

One month after assuming the responsibility he bore as king, he fought a pitched battle against two Viking armies. The outcome was again indecisive. From this Alfred concluded he could not prevail militarily at this time and the Vikings concluded they could not easily defeat him. So Alfred paid a monetary tribute for the Vikings to leave Wessex and they accepted this for the time being. His allies on his northern border, the Mercians, did the same.

The invaders were unfaithful partners to the agreement, at least twice over the next few years again threatening the kingdom. Alfred again chose to buy them off with a financial tribute, but also negotiated that they each leave high ranking hostages with the other to guarantee their word. Alfred desperately needed time to strengthen his position.

In 878, six years into Alfred's reign, the Vikings launched a third invasion in violation of their agreement. They struck without warning at the site where the court was celebrating Christmas, apparently with the intention of capturing Alfred, who had become the backbone of the organized resistance to their rule of the British Isles. Perhaps it was the Christmas celebrations. Perhaps it was the unlikelihood of an attack in the winter season. Perhaps he placed too great a trust in the truce and the hostages that guaranteed it. Whatever the reason, Alfred, for the first time, was caught completely off guard and had no more than minutes to escape capture.

A thousand years ago, England still had large areas of land that were not reclaimed from the dense forests and underbrush that grew aggressively in the wet island climate. The land had not yet been drained and ditched to make it the rich agricultural land we now know. Alfred fled into the marshlands and thickets where the invading force could not find him. Joined by a small band of men, he moved about under cover of terrain, weather and darkness, evading capture. They lived off stores taken in raids against the enemy and, when necessary, against the Saxons themselves who, in the absence of their king, had succumbed to Viking rule. You, again, will have little trouble imagining any of this.

Alfred was at the lowest point of his reign. He had dreamed that one day he would help his people rebuild the culture that had been lost to them and which lived on only in isolated monasteries. Now it seemed unlikely he would have that chance. Indeed, if the Vikings prevailed, even the remnants of Anglo Saxon civilization would be wiped out of existence

If you have ever been in England in January and February you will not soon forget how the wet cold penetrates your garments and enters your bones. And Europe in our time is in a relatively warm climatic cycle. For weeks, Alfred hid in the bitterly cold swamps of Somerset, as much at risk from the damp and frost as from the Vikings. The story has come down the generations that one day he took refuge in a swineherd's hut, no more than a simple structure of earthen floor and thatched roof. There were some oatcakes cooking in the primitive oven which, in his exhaustion, he failed to notice. When the swineherd's wife returned and found him collapsed in the hut, she berated him for failing to turn the cakes and allowing them to burn. For all the generations that followed, the story became the symbol of the wretched, desperate state in which the king found himself as he fought on to save his country. A swineherd scolding a king. As I told you, Alfred's situation much resembled yours. It could be argued that, in a land invested by a *conquering nation, he was less the king and more the chief resistance fighter.*

Alfred fortified a position in the marshes as rapidly as the weather and enemy movements allowed and began to organize resistance to the Vikings. As word spread that their young king was still alive, men from across his province secretly made preparations to join him in a surprise counter attack on the Vikings. After five months in the marshes he was ready. He sent word to those who would fight with him to join him at Egbert's Stone, a widely recognizable landmark. When he reached the rendezvous, unsure what he would find, he was met by cheering throngs of men who had gathered from the surrounding countryside to fight with him. They gave him the loyalty he had dearly earned.

Two days later, Alfred's citizen army marched to the Viking's camp in Wiltshire and prevailed in battle. He pursued them to their stronghold and lay siege. Two weeks later, now cold and hungry themselves, the Viking army sued for peace and once again promised to leave Wessex, leaving hostages with Alfred. This time, Alfred left none with them.

To seal the peace, Alfred persuaded the Viking King, Guthrum, to come with his senior officers and accept Christian baptism. How he managed this remarkable conversion is lost to us in history but we may imagine that the Vikings who asked for their own gods' help in battle, attributed Alfred's uncanny ability to survive and conquer to the power of his god. In any case, Alfred used this ceremony, not to humiliate Guthrum but to honor him and present him with gifts! We cannot help but wonder what impression this magnanimous treatment of an enemy made on Guthrum in contrast to his own ruthlessness, and how much it contributed to the relatively lengthy period of freedom from invasion the kingdom of Wessex then enjoyed.

The invading Viking armies retreated to other parts of the British Isles and, tired of fifteen years in the field, they settled down and replaced those ancient kingdoms with political structures of their own. Yet another Viking army that had already landed, upon hearing of the defeat of their countrymen, abandoned thoughts of attacking Wessex on their own. They pulled up anchor and sailed for the Continent, where they spent the next thirteen years, leaving Wessex in relative peace.

I am sure that in your hearts you are cheering the story of this fine young leader. It is a story that gives great satisfaction to those who value courage and perseverance in the face of daunting odds. But, as good as this story may be, it is only the background to the story I have yet to tell you. The story of what made Alfred great and good is only now beginning. A skillful or a lucky commander can win a war, but this alone does not make him great or good.

What made Alfred great and good is how he conducted himself during the periods of war and what he did with the precious periods of peace.

We know that the peace lasted thirteen years. Alfred, of course, had no idea as to how much time he could count on to implement his vision. Thus he wasted no time, no time at all.

His first target had to be reforming his defenses. He designed a string of fortifications carefully placed to guard the routes into Wessex. But rather than have them serve only a military purpose, he designed many of them as urban developments that could support both military and social improvement. We can imagine that they became hubs where flour could be ground, hides tanned, iron forged, tools and weapons fashioned, ideas exchanged, disputes resolved and communities brought together.

Similarly with his people. He divided his army into two so that at any given time half were home and half on duty. Not only did this ensure a food supply for the population, it won him further loyalty and minimized desertions. He was always thinking "mission" and "welfare of the people" simultaneously. You should think about this, too, because sooner or later a leader may try to convince you that the mission is more important than the people it is supposed to serve.

But this is still only what made him a good political and military leader. It is not what made him great. What made him great was one of the most remarkable acts of leadership ever conceived by a sovereign.

Alfred reasoned that it was not worth defending your land and culture unless it was a culture of which you could be proud. He knew the kingdom once contained literate men who read and taught the writings of other men who struggled with the great questions of life. Questions about the nature of man, of morals and philosophy and science. He knew this learning existed elsewhere in the world and had been lost to his own kingdom during the dark ages after the fall of Rome. He reasoned that his kingdom's vulnerability to Viking attack was at least in part due to the deterioration of its state of learning and organization. They were not simply victims of fate, but were accountable for their own insufficient vitality to withstand the assault.

So Alfred began a campaign to restore learning to his land. He appealed to the bishops of abbeys elsewhere in the British Isles to lend him teachers. He appealed to his peers abroad to do the same. He collected around him a small and diverse set of scholars whom he placed in positions from which they could restore learning throughout Wessex.

And, in the way visionary leaders act and their actions then allow their vision to further develop and unfold, Alfred went through a marvelous thought process. First he conceived that Latin, the language in which the great texts were written, had to be relearned in his land. If this was to happen, he and the senior officers of his court would have to be among the first to learn and set the example. So he and his men, all brave and illiterate, began the difficult process of mastering literacy as adults, while tending to their other critical military and civilian responsibilities.

This bold concept and personal sense of responsibility soon led him to an even bolder idea, a truly revolutionary concept for his time. Alfred reasoned that his people did not speak Latin. They spoke the English of their day. If texts could only be read in Latin, learning could not progress beyond a small circle of elites. Why not translate key texts into English and teach his people to read in their own tongue? With this radical concept, he laid the foundation for what would become the English national identity with all that it has subsequently contributed, however imperfectly, to the world. And he personally, amidst the pressing duties of governance, and self-imposed rigors of his devout religious observance, painstakingly translated four of the chosen texts from Latin into English. Talk about the leader being the model for the new order!

To create readers for these books he established a school in the court for the sons of noblemen and non-noblemen alike, determined that the next generation would be literate. Short haul, long haul. He established two religious centers, for monks and nuns, again ensuring the widespread restoration of learning. Both literacy and translated texts spread through the land in tandem.

Under the impetus of his program to restore learning, the Anglo-Saxon Chronicle was written, an extensively researched historical record that extended beyond his kingdom of Wessex to expand the sense of English identity. He propagated a code of laws to settle disputes with less bloodshed and kept a hand in ensuring they were fairly administered. The taxes he collected were shared equally between matters of defense and institutions that were the foundation of the civil and spiritual society he was building. It sounds like a fairy tale, but this is all well documented!

While Alfred built civil society, urging, cajoling and scolding his lieutenants if they dragged their feet, he continuously paid attention to the military and political, never knowing when his nemesis, the Vikings, would return. At his insistence, ships were built to meet their ships, as armies had been organized to meet their armies. And return they did. But this time Wessex was ready and the Vikings met well-organized resistance at every turn. When they threatened to sail up the Thames from London, in the kingdom of Anglia which they controlled, Alfred acted. He invested London which the Vikings had held and drove them out. With this great symbolic victory, laid upon the foundations of a national identity he helped create, Alfred was recognized by all parts of England that were not under Viking control as the "supreme" leader who would coordinate their efforts. In a sense, England had been born.

If there was ever a man who used the power he acquired in his life effectively, it was Alfred. King Arthur is the mythic figure of old England but King Alfred was the real thing. While his military achievements were the turning point for Anglo-Saxon civilization, it was his deep respect for life and learning which won him the heart of history herself. The illiterate, youngest son, afflicted with a mysterious disease, whose very survival had been in doubt as he lay shivering in the swampy winter countryside, transformed himself and, by his example and leadership, transformed his country. What he could not know is that, by his acts, he influenced the development of much of the world for the next thousand years.

Alfred's failing, if it could be called such, was being caught in the paradigm of monarchy. It would be up to other reformers and revolutionaries, hundreds of years beyond his own moment in history, to break this paradigm and replace it with non-hereditary institutions.

INTERLUDE:
Lament

It is a shame that I have to die soon. It seems that I have come to understand so much recently. I wonder what I might come to understand if I could live to one hundred and fifty. In good mental health, of course.

Perhaps I would be able to discover the answers to questions that have eluded mankind. Answers to why some men are cruel, why wars are so frequent, why prejudices are so hard to eradicate.

I know this is the wishful thinking of an old man. I have learned that some questions have no clear answers, no permanent solutions. That there can only be processes of continual struggle, of passing the torch generation to generation to individuals who will form groups that struggle to create the best conditions possible in which people can live justly. Still, I can dream. I can dream of a world I will not see, but maybe, someday, someone will see.

I have never been afraid of death. I have been much more afraid of grave injury leaving me incapacitated. But, neither do I welcome death, as it will rob me of two things I treasure.

The first theft will be of my ability to experience the future. The future is always exciting to me. What changes will occur that we cannot even imagine now? What new ways will be discovered of feeding people, healing people, communicating, traveling, and seeing the world at the grand level of the galaxies or the invisible level of the atomic nucleus? Without seeing the future, we will not even know what our own children will become, how their lives will turn out, what contributions they will make. Death will rob me of knowing any of this.

The second theft will be of what I can give to the world. I have always measured the worth of my life by what I can give to others. I always wish I could have given more – that I was smarter, or had more endurance or more resources with which to help others. Death will ensure that I can give no more. This is why I am hurrying to cheat death. If I can finish writing this while my eyes and mind are working and my heart still beats,

I will leave something through which I can continue to give. To you who are reading this. To others you may share it with.

I enjoy the idea of cheating a thief. It is just deserts. It has how I felt when we took on thugs who called themselves rulers. They deserved to have stolen from them their phony facades of respectability, their sleep at night and the armies which kept them in power.

I confess that those were the most exciting days. The days of glory, whatever the hardships. The days in which I felt so much more alive than the rest of the world. More aware of things than the rest of the world. More in charge of my fate.

I also confess that I miss those days. But I realize they were addictive, like the cocoa leaves we chewed in the jungle to keep us going. I had to learn to break the habit of always struggling. I had to relearn how to live and how to enjoy the simple acts of living. I never became excellent at this, but I got better, good enough to have a sense of rejoining the human race, and not always being above it. I think it was dangerous to always feel above it.

I have learned many lessons. It always surprises me when I learn a good lesson. It keeps me feeling fresh about life. But there is not much more time for lessons. It feels that there is only just enough time to share the lessons. Except, of course, that I still must learn the lesson of how to die, but I will not be able to share that one with you. I'm sure you'll understand.

CHAPTER III:
Monsters and Revolutionary Chaos

What Makes a Monster?

Whoever chases monsters should see to it that in the process he does not become a monster himself."- Rafael Perez, a police officer who admitted to framing innocent people and lying in court.

When we look at the baby pictures of tyrants we cannot detect any trace of the monsters they became. Perhaps the greatest of all the needs of humanity if we are to finally mature as a race is to understand how monsters become political leaders or how political leaders become monsters. We do not know the answer to this critical question. We do not even know if becoming a political leader brings out the monster or if it is the monster who seeks political power.

If we knew these things we might have saved a hundred million lives in the last century from brutal, premature deaths. We can barely fathom this, it is so staggering! But the fact that we do not know the answers does not mean we cannot know something about the subject, perhaps enough to avoid the rise of a particular monster in a particular place and time. Perhaps your place and time.

Chances are that you are already fighting a monster. This is not necessarily so, as the system itself may be so corrupt that it is not driven by an individual monster. The system has made petite monsters of many. Regardless, monstrous things are occurring and, in many cases, an individual holds the supreme power who has become monstrous or who tolerates monstrosity.

The terrible truth I must confront you with here, is that many of these monsters, past and current, were once themselves idealistic revolutionaries. Therefore, this discussion is of the utmost importance to you. I am not necessarily claiming that they were monsters before or during the revolution. Often they were brave visionaries. But we know that many revolutionaries have behaved as monsters once the revolution succeeded.

What a terrible thought! To fear the results of the revolution's success when the revolution itself is fighting against monsters! This sounds like anti-revolutionary propaganda. A tactic to confuse. A call for inaction. It is not! It is a warning, a terrible trumpet alerting all that the dangers of victory are as great as the dangers of defeat. We must think now how we will deal with victory if it is a victory worth winning and a victory worth killing and dying for.

History is not offering us one or two aberrations as examples. The recently past twentieth century strew the ground with bloody examples, making them almost a terrible normality. Leaders who people depended on to lead them along a new path, somehow turned that path into an autobahn to hell, studded with mass graves, starved children, midnight knocks at the door, weeping dungeons, instruments of torture and the bones of those who died screaming and broken. If we cannot know the ultimate answer to how this occurs, what can we know about it? What can you do about it so your own revolution and its revered leaders stay true to their vision, to the vision for which you fight? So they do not succumb to this other force whose nature we have yet to clarify?

The place to start is within ourselves. There is apparently a small egg or seed of a monster within each of us. This may not be absolutely true, but it is true of many of us. There are different theories about this egg, some religious, some evolutionary, some biochemical. We do not know which theories have merit. Nor do we know how this egg becomes fertilized, how it begins to develop. Biographies of monsters always search for this. It seems always to be an individual story. A father who did this. A mother who did that. A beloved brother who was killed for his reformist beliefs, setting off an unquenchable thirst for revenge. In hindsight we can always piece together some sort of story to explain what we urgently need to understand. But these are stories told in hindsight and rarely do us good now.

I submit to you, my brave revolutionary, that you must assume that the egg is there within each of us and most especially within yourself. You can picture it if you wish. Give it a shape and color. Feel its weight and texture and temperature. Smell its faint, ominous odor. In your mind, make it look like something real because, though invisible, it is as real as the DNA which shapes every aspect of your body. Recognize that within that egg, lays all the monstrosity the world has known, and under the right conditions it may be incubated, hatch, and seize control of you. Given the wrong influences, the right opportunity, a certain amount of power, and it could hatch within you and use your own life force to sustain and grow the monster that lay dormant in its sac.

So we learn how to abort the birth of monsters by first looking within ourselves and recognizing that monsters within are as dangerous as the monster without, and more insidious. Somehow, the Trojan horse has entered our gates and hid within our walls, waiting for the right moment to reveal itself and destroy us. Just as under colonialism and neo-colonialism, self-hate entered our hearts and formed a layer under our skins. The great battle we must fight is to recognize that the enemy is within us, that we must not externalize it onto others. Even if our philosophy tells us this enemy is reactionary thinking, or Manichean thinking, or Satan or a jinni or voodoo, it is still within us and the battle must be fought within and not be erroneously displaced onto others.

We must summon the greater power we have, whether we view this as rationality, or will, or God and the prophet of God, or our fundamental sense of morality. We must summon this power and use it to own the other power that is within us and has become a part of us. By seeing it is a part of us, and recognizing that the part cannot be stronger than the whole, we can relegate it to its place as a potential that we will not allow to manifest. We must do this ourselves through personal responsibility and, at the same time, we must use whatever means of support are at our disposal culturally to help us do this. We can pray, we can fast, we can seek counseling or guidance, and we can utilize communal self-criticism or share our darkest fears with a trusted comrade. However imperfectly we prevail, we must prevail.

I want you to stop now and find this egg! If your revolution is important to you, as I know it is, I want you to stop right now and do your best to find it within yourself.

Get a picture in your mind's eye. It does not matter whether the picture is clear or flimsy. Just do your best. Then locate a spot in your body where this imaginary egg might lay hidden. See it lying there, hidden, undetected, waiting for the right conditions. I'm serious. Close your eyes and keep them closed until you can imagine this egg within you. Then you can open your eyes again and turn the page.

Now that you can imagine this egg, imagine the conditions that would incubate the egg in you. Would the brutal death of those you love the most fertilize the egg? Would the power to wreak vengeance on those who did you wrong fertilize it? Would unlimited access to secret bank accounts and sexual orgies provide the spark? Would the taste of power that comes with torturing another trigger a pleasure center in your brain more addictive than a drug? Would paranoia that others were coveting the power you had gained begin the relentless growth of the monster in the egg? Would working day and night, year after year, thinking of nothing else but gaining power hatch the monster? Would being surrounded by people who did your bidding whenever you raged at them, teach the monster to grow more fierce? There are some combinations of conditions which are favorable for the gestation of this egg that you must become aware of and monitor.

Please, my sons and daughters, take time now to close your eyes and discover what potential is in you. Sit quietly for a while. Contemplate this. Then you can begin reading again. It is more important that you learn about yourself than you read my words. They will just be empty if you do not use them to learn about yourself.

Thank you for the courage to explore your own potential for evil. This is the same courage we are asking of society, to explore and understand its own evil. Only then can it transform and cease being the unjust thing it has become. It all starts with the courage to see the parts of ourselves that are not attractive, that we would rather disown. To strip away the superstructure that tells us we are good, and to admit that we are partly good and partly not good. Only then can the process of choice about changing things begin.

Now we can embark on the next leg of the journey. If there are conditions that are favorable to awakening the malevolent spore, then there are surely conditions that are unfavorable to doing so. What are they? This is an urgent question that must be answered by each individual who is accruing power. What are the conditions you can create that are toxic to monster eggs, which suffocate them in the womb?

The desirable conditions are undoubtedly different for each individual. Imagine what they are for you. Is it to pray for humility every night? To pray to be able to forgive the terrible transgressions against you and your loved ones? To work with the sick and dying to learn and relearn humility? To laugh with young children? To read philosophy? To gather people around you who are not afraid of you? To read the history of despots and the fate they meet by their contemporaries or by the unintimidated pen of history? Is it to create a system in which no one can have dominant power? Is it to imagine your death six months from now and how you would want to be remembered? Is it to resign your command when you feel the egg straining to hatch, before the monster emerges to devour you?

By wrestling with the terrible truth of the monster egg within ourselves, we can sense the power it can attain over our leaders and their lieutenants. We do not want to lose our revered leaders or loyal right hand men to this enemy that attacks from within. But until we let ourselves grasp the power of the monster within the egg once it hatches and matures, we will not inoculate them early enough to make a damn of difference. The monster will hatch and quickly grow through adolescence and harden into its ugly, fully-grown form. At that point it will simply eat anything in its path and will not stop until it is killed by something stronger than itself or by the ultimate leveler, time.

If we understand the corrosive nature of this egg, of the terrible growth of the hatchling, we would pour the remedy down the leader's throat as quickly as we would administer quinine for malaria. Even if he struggled, we would not hesitate to inoculate him against a wildly infectious disease that threatened him and his whole country. If we knew it would save his health, his life, his people, his good name, then out of our respect for him, out of love for him, we would administer the prevention needed.

If we have begun with ourselves, by confronting the potential monster within us, we can face others without seeking to become their police, their judges or their executioners. We can be their loyal followers and help ensure they continue to earn our loyalty. We are all imperfect agents of change, all potential carriers of the virulent egg, and all fellow protectors of the revolutionary ideal.

Ah, there is that word – ideal. Remember always, an ideal is something we strive for. It is rarely, if ever, something we reach. We are not ideal.

Our leaders are not ideal. Our revolution is not ideal. It is not treasonous to recognize in which ways we or our leaders fall short of our ideals. All along the way, we depart in greater or lesser degrees from the ideal. This is not shameful. It is human. It only becomes shameful if we cease learning from our departures, cease striving for our ideal, while insisting that others live by the ideal. Then we become hypocrites and hypocrites are deeply shameful and have to hurt or destroy others to hide their shame.

And remember this: the food, the fertilizer, the nourishment of monstrous eggs is power and the craving for power. This is the great paradox of revolutions. All revolutions seek to redistribute power. Our leaders need greater power to achieve their revolutionary goals. Without power they cannot combat evils, cannot create justice. It is our duty to help them acquire power. Our goal. Yet by this very act we expose them to the dangers of the monster in the egg awakening.

As we are successful, as we acquire the power to command the world's attention, to bring the repressive regime to the bargaining table or send it fleeing into exile, as we mobilize the masses in the street, as all the things come to pass for which we have given everything, the egg begins to awaken. Our greatest moments of triumph contain the seeds of the greatest threat to our ideals and dreams. This is the paradox to which every revolutionary must stay aware.

As power is attained a dangerous cycle ensues. Those who acquire some earthly power enjoy its taste. They exercise it, as they should, for power must be used. They experience the satisfying sensation of strength and utilization one feels when exercising muscles. The sensation encourages them to use the power more and, in doing so, they find it even more enjoyable. A deep pleasure center is activated in their brains where the acquisition of power is a key evolutionary strategy. It is so intensely enjoyable that we might surmise it acts like a drug, and the beginnings of craving for the drug can be seen or felt.

It is at this point that a vicious cycle can begin. Those who taste power may now begin to fear losing it, perhaps as an addict may become anxious about losing his supply of drugs. They may begin to act differently in small ways to keep their power and, unwittingly, begin feeding the egg. Their small actions are less pure than actions they previously took. They are aware of this, though they push the awareness to the periphery of their minds. They are aware, though they will not admit so, that their impure acts injure others.

Now, we can surmise, another cycle pursues. They fear retaliation if the other whom they have injured acquires his own power. So they are prone to further injure the other to weaken his ability to retaliate. And, if they do, they become more fearful of retaliation. The egg grows. If not interrupted, the cycle continues spiraling. The egg enlarges and eventually reaches the point of hatching. If the cycle is not broken soon, the egg reaches its full size and bursts open, spawning virulent creatures all around its breeched shell.

Some of the great thinkers on this subject go even further. I have sought out the thinkers on this subject for decades, so desperately have I wanted answers to this phenomenon I have observed. How to explain the horrifying phenomenon of the millions of deaths at the hands of those who started off to free their people of oppression – my friends V.I. and Uncle Joe "The Eagle of Georgia", Chairman Mao, Pol Pot? And these are just the more famous.

The great social anthropologists Ernst Becker and Elios Cannetti speculate that behind this behavior is the deeply buried fear of death we all carry within us, that desperately seeks a way to avoid the fate that lies in wait for every human being. The fate of death, of personal extinction. The fear that we will pass from life with no trace. That at some point we will be unremembered, our lives will be unmarked. According to these thinkers, this primal fear will cause us to do anything to escape the terrible feeling of dread it instills. It causes us to not just seek power over others, but to seek ultimate power, the power of life and death. And not just to claim this power, but to exercise it again and again and again in a desperate effort to demonstrate that it is not we who are death's victims. We are death's agents, its distributors. As long as we can mete out death, regardless of whether it is to our enemies or our comrades or subjects, we are obviously not death's victims. As we watch others fall, we get a deep, addictive satisfaction of seeing that we are the survivor while all others around us die.

Perhaps this is the egg. Perhaps even before we, ourselves, kill another in battle, or in a revolutionary tribunal, we see others fall around us. Even if we love them, and will miss them, we feel an unspeakable, inadmissible satisfaction deep within ourselves that we are better than they, as we have survived and they are dead. It fills us with an odd and delicious sense of power. Not being able to admit this perverse feeling in the face of our comrades' deaths, even to ourselves, the egg begins to hatch. If this sense of power feels so good, how to experience it again? And again? And again?

The cycle of fear of retaliation meshes with the cycle of addiction and craving for power, each reinforcing the other. The cycle becomes irreversible and spins out of control. First acts are garbed in revolutionary logic. Of course this one must be incarcerated or die. And that one. And these people. And those. Then, if we acquire enough power, even the need for revolutionary justification falls away and our actions become simply our actions, our expression of the power we have accrued. Until those around us begin to realize this is no longer the revolution being served, this is something else. This is a monster.

Eventually, like all cycles, it ultimately exhausts itself, if from nothing more than the old age, degeneration and death that eventually befalls the monster, despite the hellish efforts to avoid it. Or, the cycle of purges and killing generates a huge counterbalancing cycle. Others make stopping this monstrous cycle the focus of their lives, as you now are making the revolution the focus of your life. But they have left it too late and it can now take years or even generations. Meanwhile, the suffering that ensues is epic.

So much better to destroy the egg now. But the secret I search for, that I will assuredly go to my grave without finding, is how to transform the egg? How to reprogram its DNA so it comes to recognize that the escape from death that true revolutionaries seek, lies not in meting out widespread death to others, not in demonstrating one's power over their lives, but in being the birth fathers and birth mothers of a new society, a more just society that future generations laud as having broken with the age-old pattern of repression? Perhaps your generation can solve this ultimate corrupting cycle that wreaks such havoc, and replace it with the virtuous cycle that creates a better world. I would rest more easily in my grave if I somehow heard that you are successful in this.

But whether the monster-making cycle is solvable for all time or not, it is preventable in your revolution. If you understand the presence of the egg, of the signs of its fertilization, of the absolute need to insist it is aborted, or to deny it the power it requires to grow, you can keep it from consuming the work to which you are dedicating your life. We do not have all the answers on how to remove the egg or prevent it from incubating. But I know the non-answer and will share it with you now. The non-answer is to do nothing. To love or fear your revolutionary leader so much that you, the earliest observers of the growth of the egg, do nothing to insist the leader recognize its dangers. This is the non-answer.

Confronting this matter requires great character and courage but you can do it. First, you try everything in your power to get the revolutionary comrade whose egg is hatching to see it, to understand it, to use his sense of higher purpose and his will to discipline the egg, to contain it or starve it so it withers. Simultaneously, you work to establish group mechanisms to distribute power so you can turn down or turn off the tap that is fertilizing the egg in any one of your leaders.

But if you can't bring the leader whose egg is clearly hatching to recognize what is occurring, to agree to limits that will stop the growth of the egg, then you must oppose the leader. The greatest mistake one can make when you are disgusted with the power grabbing behavior of one faction, is to walk out of the conference or convention and cede power to the incipient monster. You must avoid doing this at all costs. However revulsive the prospect of continuing to work with comrades who are displaying unconscionable behavior, this is the very reason you must not abandon the field to them. I am sorry to say in retrospect, the democratic wing of the party should not have walked out on V.I. It was almost as bad as Gregor Strasser walking out on the National Socialist party and leaving the field to the monster Hitler.

Find the leaders who do not show signs of the egg stirring and put all your effort behind them. They may not be as charismatic and golden tongued, but they can be trusted. Support the leaders who seem to take the power and feed it to others, who use it but do not crave it. Who understand that they serve the people and the people do not serve them.

You must do this if the revolution is to fulfill its destiny and not become another blot on the history of your suffering people. Please take it from me, you must. The stains of history should not become stains on your revolution. Do not assume someone else will take care of this. This may be your most important contribution to the revolution.

Funding the Revolution

*"If you start off by robbing banks
you end up as a bank robber."*

Forgive me. I don't remember who said this. My mind has lapses. But the saying evokes a fear in me that you should share. This is the most frightening chapter for me to write, because I have no idea what to say. Yet something must be said.

I think this quote by someone or other raises fear in me because it is stirring up an unwelcome truth. You cannot wage revolution without money and finding this money is always a problem that needs to be solved. But, so often, there is a great price to be paid for the solution.

In an ideal world, which I have never been able to find despite a century spent looking for it, the people who would benefit by coming out from under the yoke of the oppressor would provide the means necessary for the revolution. But it is never so simple. Most of these people do not have any money. They are barely getting by. Those who do have money, take the greatest risk supporting your revolution early on, which is when you most need the money and help.

Inevitably, the leaders of the revolution look around frantically for where they can get what they need. It is here that the mischief starts. Those who have the kind of money and resources you need are motivated by powerful self-interest. Perhaps they are external enemies of your country who would like to see it geopolitically weakened. Perhaps they have designs on your markets and untapped wealth. Whatever, they have their agenda, which is different than yours. You are aware of this. You are aware of the dangers. But what choice do you have? Very little, it seems.

Perhaps external powers are not sufficiently interested in your country to invest in improving their position in it. Your country is too poor. Too insignificant. What do you do then? You survey your options. There is always wealth somewhere. Perhaps it is in the mines that so insatiably orphan children. Or in the banks where a handful of powerful families horde their assets. Or in the drug trade that ruins lives. So it seems you must go into the mining business, using your force to expropriate some of the wealth of the mine operators. Or into the bank robbing business, redistributing the wealth directly. Or you demand payment to protect the drug smugglers.

Whatever you do, it is hard to keep your hands clean. Those in power who deny you political rights also have dirty hands. Filthy hands. But now, to oust them, it appears that you will get your hands dirty, too.

What can I tell you? Of what can I warn you? You are on a slippery slope to becoming a bank robber. Or worse. It is the slope on which the ideals of the revolution meet the reality of finance and power. All I can do is warn you of dangers surrounding the acquisition of money and resources. I cannot give you answers. You will have to discover the answers. In some senses, you will have to be the answers.

There is the danger of greed. An obvious source of money are the small manufacturers and shopkeepers and better off farmers. They do not have a lot, but they have something and they are easy targets in the areas you control or in which you have influence. You impose a revolutionary "tax." Your collectors are themselves the dispossessed. With rifles in their hands, they suddenly have the possibility of access to that which, in the recent past, they could only look at through shop windows whose doors were barred to them. The promise of the revolution may or may not come to pass. The opportunity of holding goods and money in the hand now may not come again. There is great temptation to extort and skim and hide. It is the seed of massive corruption that will turn the revolution into the next oppressive regime. How do you prevent this?

You can be harsh and cut off the hands of those caught stealing from the people and the revolution. Set the example. But more often than not, this is the act of scapegoating. Of trying to absolve collective guilt on the backs of a few poor individuals. People become more careful, but do not stop their practices.

If there is an answer, it is the answer of leadership. It begins with being a model for the behavior you wish to prevail. Che was scrupulous. He always issued scrip for the future repayment of what he took. Once victorious, he would forego half his modest salary as director of the national bank and reject a large, confiscated house in favor of smaller quarters for himself and his family. But even before victory, he lived and toiled on the same terms as those he lead, except when his crippling asthma demanded special consideration. You cannot overestimate the importance of being a good model. But it is not enough, and Che did not learn this.

If you yourself live purely but do not pay attention to those around you, they begin to secretly despise you as being sanctimonious, of killing the joy in life, of being holier-than-thou and making the rest feel dirty. They build elaborate charades to show you they are living in the spirit you trumpet, while spending large amounts of energy to lead their secret lives in which pleasure has a place, outside your field of vision. They count on your sanctimoniousness to keep you from looking and seeing. They are the fathers of new waves of cynicism as everyone but you begins to play the game of "how much can I get since everyone else is doing it."

As a leader, you must live according to your ideals, but not so these ideals squeeze the joy out of life. When you disown the need for pleasure, you divorce yourself from the reality of the lives of the people you lead. They need joy, they need pleasure, even if you do not. Let them see you partake, but in moderation. Let them see you acknowledge that you have self-interest as well as revolutionary interest, but in the proper balance. Then you can exhort them to do the same. To find the appropriate balance. However the money is raised, let a little of it go explicitly to their enjoyment of life so they do not need to set up subterranean cultures of extortion to satisfy their pleasures. Their lives do not then become revolutionary masks underneath which they act as thugs. They can integrate their human desire for physical pleasure with revolutionary loyalty and avoid the excesses that come when parts of the personality are driven underground and made criminal. Am I making myself clear? Do you understand what I am saying? I ask you, because I think this is such a difficult subject.

Another great danger I must warn you of is the habit of confiscation. The oppressor you fight against has, by one means or another, by inheritance or by force of his own deeds, captured control of disproportionate wealth. Through oppressive taxation that does not use the taxes raised for legitimate public services, or through other mechanisms, there is an institutionalized confiscation of wealth Those not in the oppressor's clique or favor are shut out from wealth, or even from the means of livelihood. The gross imbalance is held in place with armed force.

You come along with your revolutionary ideals and must find the resources to implement them. The amount of money you can raise is limited, even tainted. You have created an atmosphere in which the money you do raise is largely used for revolutionary purposes and not personal aggrandizement. Yet it is not nearly enough to accomplish your mission. You cast around for alternatives and see the accumulated wealth in this class, or that minority, in this industry or that sect. With the goals of the revolution in mind, with the greater good as justification, and with the power at your disposal, you confiscate part of this wealth to support your noble cause. Perhaps you issue revolutionary tender as a promise to repay the "donor." Perhaps you do not. There is a sense of cosmic redress of economic imbalance, a sense of justice in what you are doing that makes it feel like a piece of the revolution is already won, is already occurring.

I am not saying that you are right or wrong. I am saying that you are in danger and your revolution is in danger. Why?

Perhaps I can best illustrate the point by telling you a fact about honeybees. It is not as far fetched as it sounds. As you know, bees are hard working creatures. We say 'busy as a beehive' for good reason. Every day, when the weather permits, bees are out doing their good work of pollinating crops while building up stores of honey for their own communal welfare. They are almost modeling your revolutionary ideals! But sometimes a bee will discover a source of already processed sugars. Perhaps a farmer's crude candy-making apparatus for his children where sugar is crystallizing on strings hung in open jars. Perhaps another beehive where the honey has already been produced and stored.

This errant bee finds it easy to return to these sources where much of the work has already been done to process raw materials into sweet forms of energy. The bee ceases to pollinate the fields and contribute to the world. Instead, it becomes a parasite, taking the fruits of other's labor and expropriating it for itself. The bee soon becomes intractably bound to this way of life. It becomes a compulsive robber of other hives. Those whose toil is being robbed become alert to the parasite and organize themselves to put an end to its ways, to kill it and once again retain the fruits of their honest labor.

So it is with revolutions. At first, confiscating the wealth of the oppressive class or its sympathizers seems fully justifiable. A minor redress of decades or generations of wrong. Then, as power accrues to the revolution, it becomes a convenient and expedient way of acquiring the resources needed to finance what still needs to be done. It frees the leadership from the need to develop other sustainable sources of revenue, sources based on an exchange of services that it provides according to the values of the revolution. Ultimately, confiscation moves from expediency to dependency. This is the only way the revolution knows to acquire the resources it needs and demands. And at that moment, it has become the oppressor.

Whatever else a revolution does, it must also focus on creating the conditions for the generation of goods and services that the people it serves need and desire. It must work out how to be a contributor to the complex process of wealth generation and distribution, and not an insatiable confiscator. This is true of any form of government, at any time and place. All governments, by their inherent design, use implicit or explicit force to confiscate a certain amount of wealth and distribute it for private or public good. Those that become addicted to confiscation, that siphon off many times more than they contribute to the common welfare, kill the goose that is laying the eggs. When the stench of dead goose becomes too much, when it fills the barnyards and courtyards and factory yards, the people rise in protest against the revolution, just as the revolution once rose in protest of the oppressors.

The last danger that comes with funding the revolution is, of course, the problem of bedfellows. They have deep pockets and approach you expressing interest in your cause, or give you a sympathetic audience if you seek them out. You know they are courting you, seeking favors for reasons of their own. They want to be your lovers in this venture, but one night you may wake up with them sticking it in your ass!

What can I say about this? Revolutionary leaders are wily. They are foxes. They are not naive about the risks they are taking. They are desperate. Better to crawl into a culvert with this snake, than to let the hounds catch them and tear them to pieces! They will deal with the snake later.

There is not much to be said. Every case is different. The risks are different. Leaders must take risks or they are not leading. They must have confidence that they can navigate the treacherous waters ahead, or at least have a reasonable shot at doing so. They can't go back. They can't avoid the upcoming rapids.

Often, they are masters at juggling factions and mutual enemies. They elicit support from diverse sources that keeps one balanced against the other. At times it seems they are performing this balancing act on a high wire a hundred feet in the air. It requires great faith to watch your leaders do this as you hold your breath and hope they don't teeter to the right or left and fall to their deaths, ripped apart at the bottom of the ravine by sharp rocks and hungry vultures.

Yet this is probably all the leader can do and the best the leader can do. To the degree he is balancing several competing interests, playing them against each other, ensuring that none attain inordinate power over him and the revolution, he is using the great principle of diversification to avoid the accumulation of power that may turn on the revolution and crush it at the very moment of its apparent victory. It is only important that you and he remember this principle when the revolution is finally won, and that you use it within the revolution itself to prevent it from being captured by one element, to the detriment of all others.

This is the best I can offer you. These are my best thoughts. It is like yelling to a man on the tightrope: "Be careful of the wind!" What good does it do? Yet, he must be careful of the wind.

Dehumanizing and Demonizing

I have told you at the very beginning that I lived through a very difficult century. So many of the great leaders, some of who I personally put my deepest faith in, caused the deaths of millions of people whose lives they were supposed to better. Joe Stalin, Chairman Mao, Pol Pot. (I still cannot bring myself to include the name of The Fuhrer in the same sentence, as there was never a vision to improve anyone's life, only a vision to conquer or eliminate other races.) So many black leaders in Africa joined these ranks. I had so much hope for Africa when colonialism began to unravel at sensational speeds in the fifties and sixties. I didn't understand then, how much of the colonialist's arrogance had been transferred to African leaders themselves.

Whether African or Asian or European, these leaders, this gallery of heroes, in my mind became villains. I am sorry if you are offended by this characterization. Old men don't care who they offend. But, nevertheless, I admit that these fallen heroes of mine did not put to death thousands or millions of people with their own hands. Somehow, they created the conditions in which others did these unforgivable deeds that drowned their revolutions in tears. It is vital we try to understand how this occurred. You want to be the cultivators of a new society, not of killing fields.

This is how I see it. A political leader must, of course, lead. He must visualize a different future and convince others it is desirable and attainable. To do that he must clearly differentiate the present from the future. Often, he paints the present darker than it is and the future brighter than it can actually be, in order to fire up people to work towards bringing that glowing future into existence. He attributes causes to the failures in the present that people can understand, whether those are the true or complete causes. To do this, he simplifies reality. This is not a bad thing in itself. It is effective communication.

The problem begins when he moves from blaming flawed or corrupt systems and policies for the people's suffering, to blaming classes of people. As soon as he blames classes of people, landowners, Humus,

Jews, whomever, he has shifted the energy of the revolution from legitimate anger to illegitimate hate. Anger is natural and necessary. It is the energy which fuels the revolution. Hate is manufactured and illegitimate. It never produces better conditions. It produces nightmares.

This was a point on which Che and I disagreed when he was getting ready to leave Cuba. He was speaking to the Tricontinental Congress. I somehow saved the transcripts from this for all these years. In his speech he called for "a long and cruel global confrontation to bring about the destruction of imperialism." He recited the qualities that would be required for this battle, including: "Hatred as an element of the struggle, a relentless hatred of the enemy, impelling us above and beyond the natural limitations man is heir to, transforming him into a violent, effective, seductive and cold killing machine..." He claimed that "A people without hatred cannot vanquish a brutal enemy."

Even now, these words make me shudder. But I never knew with Che as he was always changing, trying to become a better revolutionary. He was so afraid of compromising the revolution as he saw so many inclined to do after winning in Cuba. I think he sometimes spoke and acted in extremes that he believed when speaking them, but which weren't his deepest beliefs. In this case I know this is true because we also have the famous letter in which he wrote: "Let me say, at the risk of looking ridiculous, that the true revolutionary is guided by feelings of love."

But that is my point. He resorts to speaking in extremes. When people who look up to a leader hear him speaking this way, they take it very much to heart. And the leader, without laying a hand on anyone directly, becomes responsible for killing far and wide throughout his land. In Che's case, because he was not the supreme leader, because he did not often speak directly to the people, we cannot lay this charge at his doorstep. But if he had lived, if he had been successful elsewhere and continued to resort to this rhetoric, if he became a leader who spoke directly to the people instead of to other revolutionary leaders, he, too, may have had this blood on his hands. Chairman Mao was not there when villagers taunted and beat to death fellow villagers who happened to have a little education or slightly more wealth than they did, but his words were there, his incitement to hate was in the fists that held the sticks.

Oppression occurs when, for whatever reason, the oppressor stops seeing his victims as human beings. When they are chattel, when they are subjects, when they are a means of harvesting the fields, of running the factories, of fighting his wars and no more. The oppressor does not see them as human beings like himself with feelings, aspirations and rights, anymore than he sees the cattle in the field this way. That is why the oppressor must be resisted and replaced. It is also why you must not become the oppressor.

It is very handy to have some class of people to demonize. It is as good as having sticks of dynamite when you are trying to get something going. But if you throw this particular dynamite you are in great danger of becoming the next oppressor. So, how do you whip up the people without whipping up hatred? Without unleashing the makers of killing fields?

You stay focused on the system, the policies, the acts that oppress people. You whip up support to change these. To eradicate and replace these with a more humane system. You whip up a demand for change. Not hatred. It is harder to do this. Do it anyway and make sure your leaders do it.

Avoid the temptation to demonize and to whip up hatred like the plague. It is a plague. Don't start it and don't spread it. Wince if you hear your leader do this. Get to him and get him to stop. Do not let this genie out of its bottle. You will not be able to squeeze him back in it. Crowds respond to calls for hatred. They roar. The roar gives them a sense of power. So they roar louder. If the leader plays this card and the crowd roars, he interprets this as adulation. He has found a switch. So he pulls it again and gets more adulation. The leader and crowd are now feeding each other. They do not realize the food is a first class poison.

A leader who plays the hate card is unwittingly making a pact with the devil. He is releasing the devil's minions. They will invest your streets and houses and villages. It will take at least two generations to pry them out again, to send them back to the nether world. They will ruin your children's and their children's lives.

Do not allow the revolution to be perverted and disfigured by hatred. Do not spend its vital energy creating classes of villains. Tear down what must be torn down and build what must be built. But do not dehumanize and demonize. Do not foment mindless retribution. Spend the revolution's energy on painting visions of futures worth living in and building systems to support those visions. Fan the sparks of hope, not hate. Do the work of the angels. That is whose side you are on. Let the devil do his handiwork in hell. Don't do it for him on earth. I have seen too much of this. I do not want it seen on earth again, even if I will not be around to have to see it myself.

INTERRUPTION:
Fright

I had a little scare this week. I got very ill for a few days. The fever ran high. My head pounded so badly I couldn't keep my eyes open if there was light in the room. I couldn't focus enough to read, let alone write notes.

I was afraid that maybe I had waited too long to do this project. That I was going to have to leave you fragments of writings, rather than a completed book. That there would be no time to ask the younger friends I have made to help me polish the manuscript and remove any glaring errors. I suppose you would forgive me some errors here and there, but I would rather find and correct them first.

For me it is a scary thought to die suddenly, just when I have something important to say or to do. Of course, I have had to live with this thought much of my life, as you must when you are being tracked down or are preparing a military action.

I suppose you have developed tricks for reducing this fear like I did. Always having a farewell letter tucked in my uniform and another in my boot and another in a bedroll. My thoughts were macabre, but not unrealistic. If I got killed by a landmine, the letter in my chest might survive. If a mortar blew away my top, maybe someone would find the letter in my boot when they went to salvage it. Or maybe the bedroll would protect the letter if my whole body was shattered. Of course, comrades always kept such letters for each other, but I wanted to increase the odds that something remained should our whole patrol be wiped out.

It seems even more pressing now. It's not a matter of surviving this battle or this year. Whatever event I manage to survive, it will not be for long. I want to tuck copies of my final thoughts about revolution in a hundred different places so someone finds a copy everywhere where revolutions are being fought.

I wonder if revolutions will need to be fought forever. Will there always be places on earth where non-revolutionary means for change are shut off by strongmen? Or by henchman of unjust, entrenched systems? It seems necessary to at least be able to imagine a world in which it is possible that revolution is no longer necessary. I find it very difficult to do that, but I am determined, even at this late stage, to at least imagine glimpses of such a world. You know and I know, the only way a better world can come into being is if it first can be imagined. If it can be imagined, then we are left with the problem of how to get there. But without being able to imagine it, there's no "there" to get to.

Forgive me. I am straying again. My point is simply this: I do not have much time. I hope that I can leave you a completed book. If I can't, please accept that which I was able to leave you in the time left to me.

Power, Sexuality and Sadism

Having lived to write another day, I will discuss a subject that many would prefer I did not. It is the dirty side of war and, therefore, sometimes the dirty side of revolution. These are the acts for which no one gets medals and for which few are ever court martialed. One chap did get his penis cut off by a hellcat of a woman and probably deserved it, but that's another story!

Revolutions are about wresting power away from those who are abusing it, or who are hoarding it for their cronies, and not sharing it with others who have a right to live decent lives over which they have a good deal of say. They are about creating public freedom, the right to live by your beliefs, and the opportunity to make the best of life that individuals and communities can make. They are not about you, personally, getting power. But, if you throw your hat into the ring, and pick up a gun, and start prowling around the countryside, you immediately have a certain amount of power.

No one fully understands the relationship of power and sex. We all know there is some sort of relationship. There has to be if the theories of evolution have any truth to them. (I don't fully subscribe to them myself, mind you, but I'd be an old fool to refute the whole subject.) If species are designed to survive, and one of the mechanisms for assuring survival is the fact that powerful males get to impregnate more females than their less powerful rivals, there is a relationship between sex and power.

Now this is theory. I've been observing powerful men for nearly a century and in practice it doesn't always work out that way. Often it does, but not always. V.I. wasn't a womanizer. Neither was Che, though he had his wife and then his mistress who became his next wife. They both channeled so much of their energy into the revolution that they weren't as interested as other men in sex, or so it seemed to me.

But a lot of other men involved in revolution weren't slowed a bit on the sex front. If anything, they were fueled by it. Maybe they weren't as serious revolutionary thinkers as V.I. and Che. I don't know, but it seemed that way. In any case, you put a gun in their hand, and send them out in the countryside without their own women nearby, and you have a recipe for things happening.

Of course, that's where discipline comes in. Che was pretty adamant about these things. He did not want the peasants outraged when he depended on them for food and intelligence. If the girl falls for you, with your beret and beard and gun in your hand, that's one thing. But don't be vague about whether she's interested or you're forcing her. You might pay with your life for endangering the revolution.

As usual, it's leadership that sets the tone. And, too often, it sets a bad tone or turns a blind eye. Their men with guns begin to force themselves on women, even on young girls. There is something intoxicating about exerting this power, some alchemy occurs when mixing sex and power. A part of the pleasure center of the brain gets stimulated that isn't usually reached. More of evolution's wiring. The drive is overwhelming.

There are some pleasures that should not be sampled for they drive a man crazy, they take over and ruin his life, drain it of any good or worth. There is heroin. There is excessive alcohol. There is rape. Why do you think men who rape, rape again? And again? Like a drug addict, men exposed to these strange and overpowering pleasure centers in their brain crave more, will do anything to get the "high" again. Their power of choice over their actions erodes. Their behavior becomes uncontrollable if anything gets in their way.

Of course, the men to whom women are attached – fathers, brothers, husbands, even sons – will not stand idly by while their women are taken. They fight tooth and nail. So the predator now has to not just display his power, but use it. Adrenaline is pumping. He slashes and stabs and beats and riddles the bodies of the men who would protect their women. Or he causes them to cower and then humiliates them in the most shameful ways. As part of this action, without a break or pause, he executes his original intention and has sex with these women in all sorts of ways, all social inhibitions removed. The stimulation and hormones and feelings of raw power and animal satisfaction get mixed together into a narcotic cocktail that he has never experienced. He is hooked and a sadistic rapist is born.

When this happens in war, you no longer have a soldier. A soldier by definition is disciplined. You have a marauder, a thug, a hooligan. When this happens in revolution, you no longer have a revolutionary. A revolutionary, by definition, is fighting for greater justice. This man has become a perpetrator of injustice.

If he is low on the totem pole he will wreak limited havoc. The lives of the unlucky people who fall into his hands will be ruined. It is expected that before this goes on too long, his comrades or field commander will put a stop to it. The revolution cannot be marred with his deeds.

But if he is high on the totem pole, he may wreak widespread destruction, slowly, carefully hidden from view. The danger he poses to human decency may not become fully apparent until the revolution has succeeded and he is put in charge of security or pacification or reeducation. Forcible sex and sadism are brothers. He will set up a chamber of horrors with the authority of the revolution supporting him, even as the oppressors did who so many died to overthrow. He will lure others into his degeneracy by exposing them to the intoxication of power and torture and sex. They will become accomplices, enforcers and psychological slaves. Like drug addicts who need bigger doses to reach their high, they will need to go to greater and greater extremes of cruelty and coercion to achieve their own arousal. The screams of their victims will be heard through nine-foot walls, hundreds of meters away.

Excuses will be given. "We are interrogating subversives." "We are punishing collaborators." "We are intimidating those who would give the enemy support." "We are avenging injustice." They are all excuses. There is great mental and moral sickness underneath the weak excuses.

You have no choice if you are to save the honor and good name of your revolution. You must preclude sadistic behavior before it starts. You must shut it off if it begins. You must isolate it if it has taken root. You must exterminate it if it resists and persists. The revolution itself is at stake.

One act of sadistic cruelty begets a thousand times that the tale is told. The grisly image that is burnished in the minds of those you seek to win over, eclipses all attempts to win trust. Do not allow a sadistic act to go unpunished. Send a message to the perpetrator that he will never forget. It is the only way you will save him as a useful revolutionary. Do not allow a confirmed sadist to retain any power within your movement. Expel him or limit him to roles in which he wields no power and is under the command of someone not afraid to exert discipline.

Sex is sex and must not be allowed to become torture. Sex is a fact of life and a fact of armed struggle. There are no pristine answers to its place in armed struggle. Che used to fret when his men slipped off to the whorehouses where they picked up disease, or informers could pick up hints of his movements. But unlike conventional war, it was too risky to allow camp followers who would slow us down or give away our location with telltale signs. And there were too few female revolutionaries to satisfy all the men, which created more problems than it solved in camp.

The best to hope for was that young girls in the countryside were attracted to the daring of the men in our ranks and, frankly, could ignore the smell the fighters acquired from months without clean clothes and baths. Friendly liaisons kept the men from becoming irritable and combative with each other. But the danger always lurked in the patrol, out of sight of its officers, as to how the men would behave if attraction alone failed.

I, who cannot even get it up anymore, and have not been able to for almost as long as some of these young men have been alive, half-cynically say "take more baths." Make yourselves more attractive. You are already lean and hard and intense, which women find desirable. Now, make sure if they close their eyes that they can distinguish you from a goat!

I make light because, as with so many of these issues, there are not easy answers. But there are clear dangers and clear wrongs. Stop the wrongs when they are small and they will not become crimes.

Maybe I feel compelled to speak of these things because I am an old man. For all I know, there are as many women in revolutionary groups now as there are men. Maybe sex will take care of itself in mixed cadres. Maybe there will even be more tolerance for sex between men, like there is in jail. I read about these things, but don't know about them.

If you are a religious revolutionary I am offending you by talking about this. I am sorry as I do not mean to offend. I mean to warn.

I am simply like the lighthouse, cautioning you to stay clear of danger. Avoid the rocks that sink even worthy ships and sailors.

Maria

Jorge repacked his bedroll, checked his ammunition belts, filled his water bags and placed his precious field glasses in his knapsack. He was preparing for a maneuver as he had done so many times before.

He knew it was not in the revolutionary spirit to do so, but he discreetly touched the cross on his neck and asked for protection.

He was headed north this time. Supplies were badly needed. They had gotten word of a convoy that would pass in two days time. He and his small troop were to intercept it. He prayed it was not a trap.

Jorge was not sorry to be going on this foray. The time spent in camp became so tedious. It was good to be going into action. Besides, there was another reason he was glad.

It had been too many nights now that he lay on his cot, unable to sleep. He had slept alone too many nights. Quietly, so as not to disturb others or be embarrassed, he took care of himself. But it was no longer enough.

In the direction to the north was the village of Peublito. He had passed through there once before. Maria had been working at the edge of the fields that day when she spotted him.

At first she froze. She had good cause to be wary of these dirty men with guns. Bandidos or Revoltosos? Bandidos were big trouble. With Revoltosos you never knew. The villagers called them revoltosos –troublemakers or rebels– instead of revolucionarios, because you never knew.

Jorge saw her and also froze. Who else was there? Were he and his men in danger? He ordered them to fan out to avoid being an easy target. With his field glasses he carefully surveyed the hillside.

This woman seemed to be alone. This wasn't smart, but he understood. There were not so many hands to go around and the work needed to be done. Risks were part of everyday life.

Jorge stood up and approached the woman. He made a sign that indicated revolucionario. He knew she wouldn't trust this as bandidos also made the sign to reassure their quarry before attacking. Maria stayed frozen. There was no point in running if they meant trouble.

When he came close he saw that she was modestly pretty. He also saw she hid her left arm in her blouse. It was his turn to freeze.

Jorge raised his gun and ordered her to remove her hand from her blouse. There was no way of telling what weapon it held.

Maria hesitated then slowly pulled her arm from the folds of material. Jorge jerked in shock. The end of her forearm was a stump.

"What happened to your hand?" he asked, the circumstances dissolving any social inhibition at such directness.

"I lost it," she said, revealing nothing in her face.

"How?"

"A Revolucionario." She used the term they called themselves.

Jorge again jerked. Nothing had prepared him for such an encounter.

"Revolucionarios don't do this."

"This one did."

Jorge digested what he could of this. "What were the circumstances?" He had to know more.

"I would not comply."

"Comply to what?" This woman told little.

"With him having his way with me."

"Many men have their way with women without the woman losing her arm." Jorge felt a growing need to understand what he was seeing.

Maria saw that she must tell the story though she hated to do so.

"I tried to run away. He caught me and threw me to the ground. When he opened his pants and was entering me I managed to free my left arm. I reached down and grabbed his balls and twisted them. He screamed and threw himself off me. I tried to run but he caught my ankle and threw me down again. I saw he had his machete in his hand. In a flash he brought it down on my left arm."

Jorge felt sick. "I am sorry." He choked back his vomit. "You must hate Revolucionarios."

"I do not hate Revolucionarios."

This seemed impossible to Jorge. He still hated the government police who arrested his sister on a phony charge and gang raped her for the night they held her in prison. "Why not? How can that be?"

"There were other revoltosos were there that day." She slipped back into their own word for these men as she recalled the events she wanted to forget. "They heard me scream and ran to the spot. They got there just as he had chopped my arm. They were furious. They screamed at him, 'You animal! You pig! Look what you have done!' Two men grabbed him, knocked him out with a rifle butt and tied his arms. Two other men ran to me and held a cloth over my arm to stop the bleeding. They carried me back to my village and helped with the medical attention.

"When I was stabilized, they went to my father to apologize for their comrade. They offered to turn him over to the village for retribution. My father declined their offer. He was in shock. 'You take care of him' he said. When they left, after a little while we heard a single shot. We cannot be sure, but we believe they delivered justice.

"If it had been bandidos they would have left me to die, after making me suffer even more. There was a bad egg, but the Revolucionarios were not bad men."

Jorge was stunned by the fairness with which this woman told her story.

"If you want," she said, "you may come to our village for a meal. It is safe."

That night, after the meal, Maria made an excuse for Jorge to accompany her to the well. When they were out of earshot of others, she took his hand in hers.

"You have kind eyes. I, too, believe in what you are fighting for. I have paid my price, but you are also paying your price. It is lonely in the mountains. If you do not find my wounds too difficult to look at, we could help comfort each other."

Maria

That night they made love on the grass, in the field not far from where a Revoltoso had made havoc. Two months had passed. Perhaps tomorrow night, Jorge would be near her village.

The Mensch

Mensch is a German word meaning person or man. But its important meaning comes from Yiddish, the related language of European Jews. You often find Jews in revolutionary movements, in Europe, in South Africa, in the Americas. I suppose it goes back to their history in ancient Egypt when they revolted against their enslavement. There was certainly no shortage of Jews in the Bolshevik ranks. It's too bad that anti-Semitism kept Trotsky from succeeding V.I. after his death. Trotsky was tough, but not crude like the Eagle of Georgia. He might have led the revolution in directions that would have ensured its long-term acceptance. But it's no use second guessing history and I am straying from my point.

The Jews use the word "mensch" to mean an honorable man, a person of character. A person who will do the right thing even when it is not the easiest course of action, or when he could get away with doing less if he chose to.

In the turbulent world of revolutions, when hatreds are fueled, when factions jockey for power, when policy disagreements are personalized, when leaders with inflated egos act to cement their own power, the mensch is the individual who makes the difference between constructive action and destructive chaos.

There are big time mensches. In my book, Mandela is the biggest. But he's not the most important. You know who is the most important? YOU! You, if you'll be a mensch. Why do I say this?

Revolutions are messy. People on every side and no side get hurt. There is much suffering. The only thing that justifies this hurt and suffering is that huge amounts of both are already created by the repressive regime. The revolution is fighting fire with fire. If a blaze is consuming hundreds of homes, everyone will agree that creating a firebreak is a reasonable action, often a necessary action, even if doing so destroys a few more homes.

The revolution is creating a firebreak. It is saying to the oppressors, no more! There are consequences to your oppression! We will not tie our own hands. We will fight you with your own weapons. Do not cross this line. Stop the spread of your destruction. Burn yourself out with your corruption and hatred. You will not advance further. We will stop you and we will force your retreat!

But in fighting fire with fire, people are getting burned on every side! The mensch says to himself, "My purpose is not to create suffering. It is to relieve suffering. If I can relieve it without endangering the revolution I will do so whenever I can." He is never soft when firmness is needed. But he is not hard for the sake of being hard.

The mensch sees an enemy soldier dying. He offers a drink of water and promises to try delivering a letter to his wife when hostilities abate.

He has a pass for three days leave. But his family is not in this region and his comrade's is. The mensch gives the pass to his comrade.

Factions in the revolutionary coalition argue themselves into a stalemate. The demands of one of the coalition members are not reasonable, but they won't really hurt one's own faction. The mensch cedes the point in negotiations for the greater good.

He does not let others take advantage of him or walk over him. He stands up for his own dignity and rights. But he takes as much interest in the dignity and rights of others. Genuinely. Not in lip service.

The mensch is not necessarily a hero. His actions do not demand courage. They demand respecting others. They demand being mature, responsible and caring about others' welfare.

If the mensch gives his word, he keeps it, even if it costs him to do so.

If he makes a mistake, he says so, even if it costs him to admit this.

The mensch does the right thing despite the price he must pay. He does the right thing because it is the right thing, not because anyone will know he did it and reward him. He does the right thing even when others do not.

If he also has courage, then the mensch becomes a hero.

He sees comrades terrorizing a young girl. Quietly he says, "Comrades. This is wrong. Let her go." If they are seized with frenzy and turn on him, he holds his ground. He risks injury, death or ostracism to do the right thing. The mensch has moved to a new level and become a hero.

Heroes are awe-inspiring. They are the counterweight to monsters. If you can be a hero, I salute you. If you cannot, I understand. But in any case, be a mensch.

If your ranks are filled with "mensches" there will be no atrocities, you will not foment vendettas and you will make fighting more honorable. If you are victorious, you will make your governing more acceptable to those who resisted you.

Petite tyrants, bullies, make life miserable. Mensches make life more tolerable. They restore hope in human nature.

Have you heard of the butterfly effect? It is an insupportable theory that contains a grain of truth. It is a theory of our ability to influence the world. If a butterfly flaps its wings in Venezuela, the gentle currents it causes are self-replicating. A small wave is started, which becomes stronger and stronger, amplifying to the point that it contributes to or creates a storm over Cuba.

In some ways this theory is not so different from Che's. He marches into Bolivia with eighteen men and expects to create a revolutionary ripple effect throughout a continent. But the theory doesn't sufficiently take into account all the other forces creating different or opposite effects. Nevertheless, look at how wide the effects of Che flapping his wings!

You never know the ripple effect of small acts of kindness and consideration on your part. Perhaps they are insignificant. Perhaps they change the course of events. If there are a thousand mensches in your ranks, a thousand acts of decency each day, I have no doubt this makes a difference. Perhaps it should be called the "flock of butterflies" effect. But you can't wait for the other 999 butterflies to go first. Flap your wings now. See what happens.

I have walked the hills with mensches. I am honored to have done so. They enriched my life. I hope that I would be honored to walk with you.

The Hero

Each of you can be a mensch. Only a few of you will be heroes. Let me explain.

You are already heroes in some regards. You have chosen to take on a daunting task and are risking all you have in its pursuit. This is the stuff of heroism. Standing up to Goliath with your slingshot. You fit this bill. I am not trying to take this away from you.

But oddly enough, in your situation the true hero is not the one who stands up to the oppressor. It is the one who stands up to the revolution, to his or her own group. How can this be?

A powerful set of forces is at work. In talking to would-be revolutionaries I have already explained the journey the individual must take to reach the point of declaring their allegiance to a revolutionary group. And I have explained that once made, the individual's survival becomes inextricably linked to that group.

To some degree or another, you, my dear revolutionary, have followed this journey. Perhaps you have done so incompletely, without full awareness. Perhaps you will need to retrace and clarify some of the steps for yourself. But this is the journey you have made.

And it is precisely at this point that the great danger of revolutionary groups exists. In any revolutionary group there is a tolerance for debate over philosophy and strategy, but only within certain limits. These limits define who is a member of the group, who can be trusted and who cannot, who is a potential revisionist or, worse, a traitor. And so, as free as these groups see themselves in contrast to the oppressors, they, too, develop an orthodoxy that one challenges only at grave peril. It is here that the hero is needed.

There is too much riding on acceptance by the group for individual members to speak freely of whatever reservations, doubts or fears they may have. If they question too much, they risk being ostracized or, in extreme cases, imprisoned or killed.

This applies even to you my dear comrade. I know what you must be saying. "Élan is full of mule shit! He's never been to one of our all night sessions where people do nothing but disagree with each other! There are many times I want to strangle them for never being able to agree with each other!" You are right about this, of course. But, nevertheless, all the arguing and disagreement is still within certain bounds. It does not violate certain taboos that everyone present understands, though never mentions. If you are honest with yourself, you have probably swept certain doubts into the corners of your mind, censored certain thoughts and chastised yourself for even having these thoughts because they smacked of revisionism or compromise or were dangerously close to the position of a competing rebel group.

This is all very normal in any group and very debilitating. You can be sure that even around the conference tables of the oppressor, there are ministers who sit on dissenting thoughts you would approve of, who don't express them because they are unwilling to look "soft." Wanting to belong and be trusted exerts its own gravity on the group that restrains any radically different thoughts from escaping minds and lips. It appears that vigorous debate is occurring, and sometimes it is, but almost always within the unspoken boundaries that limit what may be thought and spoken.

The hero is a hero because he is willing to speak the unspeakable. He speaks of revolutionary thought that impedes revolutionary goals. He speaks of revolutionary policies that violate revolutionary principles. He speaks of revolutionary acts that violate the human values on which the revolution was born.

He does not speak to disrupt or derail the group, or to grab attention and power for himself. He does not speak to undermine the existing leadership. He speaks out of love for the revolution and for the values on which it is determined to build the future. If he has fear for his own welfare, he fears more for the welfare of the revolution, and speaks out.

Sometimes he is heard and exerts influence. Sometimes he is shouted down. Sometimes he is shunted to the periphery and does not return for years, until events prove him farsighted. Sometimes he never returns.

Those with less courage than the hero take pains vying to show who can display their orthodoxy louder and stronger, who is tougher and more pure in their revolutionary thought, who the leader can rely on or bear in mind as a future successor.

This plays out not just at party headquarters or policy meetings, but in the field as well. You often see macho displays of strength and toughness, acts of bravado that harm or humiliate others. A comrade who speaks out against these acts is mocked or threatened. The instinct of the pack is for conformity. The hero stands up to the pack when it is violating the values on which the revolution should be built. If he prevails, the revolution is better and stronger. If he fails, he often pays a great personal price, but not the price others pay of staining their own honor.

You may find yourself in a situation calling for a hero to stand up. Your knees may fail at the crucial moment. Your mouth may go dry. I hope you understand better the forces working against you. Perhaps it will take more time before you can overcome them and stand and speak when it is important that a voice be raised. But even now you can recognize the courage of whoever does rise and you can lend them your support. This you can do. Sometimes it is the voice who seconds the hero that turns the tide. One time, it may be your voice.

Sasha's Diary

September 7, 1920

Boots full of rain. Soles deteriorating.

Lots of talk that the White army is folding everywhere. Proud to be part of defending the revolution.

Wish feet were dry.

September 9, 1920

Feet beginning to crack between toes.

Have been ordered to V--- in Tambov province. Need for security emphasized. Not briefed on what our objective is. Not aware that White army is still active in region.

Sep 10, 1920

Traveling to V---. I have never been more grateful for any invention than the railroad. My feet would not have gotten me there. Two days in dry boxcar letting fissures between toes heal.

My men are grateful for the rest. Train rocking many of them to sleep like babies.

Sep 13, 1920, V---

We arrived today. Confusing situation. No armed reactionary forces in area. Met at station by throngs of peasants. Some angry and belligerent. Others pleading. Hard to pay attention to their concerns when I need to bivouac my men.

Rain started again.

Sep 14, 1920

Regional commander called briefing of all cadre leaders. Attempted to clarify situation. Some peasants causing trouble. Expected Bolsheviks to redistribute land. Instead, Bolsheviks demanding farmers hand over harvest to feed cities.

Orders to find and eliminate those resisting party orders.

Sep 15

Led men on house-to-house search for hidden grain. A Kulak pulled me aside to talk. Comrade Lenin warned us Kulaks are reactionary. They have more land and animals, more to lose.

Kulak bent my ear for two hours, explaining support for revolution but concern for keeping enough grain to feed own family and seed grain. Seemed reasonable.

He saw state of my boots. Offered me a fresh pair. His son had died fighting Whites when they were here. The son had small feet like mine. He's glad for me to take the boots.

Sep 18

Searching houses for three days. Unpleasant. Old women crying or screaming at us. What are we to do? Sent eight cartloads of grain back to railhead for shipping to cities. Our contribution.

Sun showed itself at last, then the clouds began pissing again.

It's my brother Alex's birthday today. He's in another regiment. Wonder what assignment he's drawn on his birthday.

Sep 19

Not a good day. Regional commander caught up with us. Warned we must be tougher. Kulaks are poisoning peasants' minds against us. Peasants are hiding grain and organizing militia. Must make some examples of troublemakers.

At least my feet are dry.

20

Commander still with us. Has begun issuing orders directly to my squad. My stomach is knotted. Feels like I'm losing control of my command.

21

I'm in shock. Do not know what to do. Who to talk with.

Commander said we must be tougher. Comrade Lenin expects it. Ordered Kulak family out of their house. Same family who gave me boots. When they came out he had us throw torches on house. The whole family began shouting in protest. Kulak's remaining son ran to throw water on fire. Commander shot him in chest. He died in his father's arms. Never saw such a look in either man's eyes.

Feel very confused. This father had already given a son to the revolution. Why now this?

22

Can comrade Lenin know what's going on? He would never tolerate it! But our commander says his orders come from comrade Lenin.

We have burnt house after house. Winter is coming. What will these people do?

Commander says peasants are now raising an army thousands strong. Why are they doing this? We are Reds, not Whites! World seems upside down.

26 —last

It's raining again. I gave my boots away as won't need them. I will be shot in a few hours as an example to other squad leaders.

We were still setting peasant houses on fire. Commander ordered me to first bar doors with the family inside. Said we needed to be tougher. Make stronger example.

I saw my wife and children's faces on this family's face. Couldn't obey. Why were we killing peasants anyway? Czarists were enemy. Refused order in front of men. Commander ordered me arrested and barred the house himself. I still hear the horrible screams. It is good I will die so I do not have to hear them for the rest of my life.

My men are slipping in to see me, saying I'm right. This is their way of saying goodbye. They are too afraid to disobey Commander.

All I ask them is to get this diary safely to my son. Want him to know. It's very confusing. Don't want to hurt revolution. But think I did right.

Wonder if I should have stopped Commander? Turned tables and arrested him? Don't know if men would have supported me. Too late to know. Think I did right.

Listening to rain on roof. I'll miss the rain.

I love my family.

Goodbye to each of you.

Support Comrade Lenin.

INTERLUDE:
How I Came To Be In North America

There must be something you are wondering. How did I come to be in the United States of America when I aligned myself against it for so much of my life?

Life is full of turns, as you know. Why was O'Higgins fighting to liberate Chile? How did San Martin come to spend the last years of his life in Brussels and Paris? Could Trotsky have predicted he would die in Mexico? Kerensky that he would live out most of his life in New York? Che that he would fight in Cuba and the Congo and Bolivia, but not Argentina?

I will be honest with you. I barely survived the era of Stalin. It was very difficult to survive in almost every way – physically, psychologically, politically. I will not belabor you with the number of close calls.

My first break came at the end of 1936 when the Comintern committed to coordinating the anti-fascists in Spain, before they began to view the Republicans as a threat to Bolshevik dominance. I was sent to Madrid as a political commissar to educate all those marvelous, hopeful volunteers on the realities of political revolution. I rubbed shoulders a lot with the Abraham Lincoln Battalion and the John Brown Battery, both of which were part of the exciting 15th International Brigade. What spirited young people!

This was my first understanding that not all Americans were pawns of the system. Here were volunteers with guns in their hands and goodness in their hearts, who sailed across the ocean to put their lives on the line against the thug, Franco. But their government, and those of the other so-called democracies, were cut from different cloth. In the pocket of corporations whose interests conflicted with democratic and humanitarian priorities, they declined to support the anti-fascist forces in the hour of the Republic's need. The thugs, with unlimited help from Hitler and Mussolini, overran the Republicans. The remnants of the doomed International Brigade limped home.

For the three years it lasted, this assignment got me out of Stalin's warped idea of a proletarian dictatorship. When I returned, we were hurled into the next horror in our lives: repelling the invasion of the German Nazi army. I will skip over the lurid details of my fight, and my countrymen's fight, to survive. We barely managed to do so and emerged thoroughly exhausted. Only the grim necessities of post-war life kept me going.

When we caught our collective breaths, the Comintern again surveyed the international landscape to determine where our resources should be deployed to greatest effect. It had been made abundantly clear by the insatiable need for oil in the war, that a choke point of the world was the Mideast.

The Comintern became determined to break the hold that the English and French had on the region. I was one of the operatives sent in to see what tensions could be exploited. I was again delighted to get out of the dismal and repressive conditions that surrounded us. Though we had defeated Hitler, I could never forget that Stalin had gotten in bed with the thug of thugs, before the Fuehrer turned and shafted him and us in the ass.

After the usual preparations, I set off for the Mideast. I set up base in Palestine. Our plans were vague and I was to look for opportunities. I roamed the region with a plausible cover. Once again, my eyes were opened. I was impressed by the intense commitment to collectivism amongst the Jewish settlers. Not a few had come from Russia and I could see the influence of the old commune system, taken to its logical conclusions. The combination of this pure, if simple form of economic communism, with direct democratic participation in governing the community, was the closest realization I had seen of the ideals for which I had fought.

Nor were these the Jews Hitler had rounded up and gassed. They had transformed themselves into warriors. I befriended the Stern Gang, who had no reluctance to use violence to shake the British overseers out of their arrogant colonialism, though Ben Gurion, the future first prime minister of Israel, had to restrain them before they alienated the sources of his support. Maintaining a balance of diplomatic and guerilla pressure, I saw Israel win its independence within a few short years, the

Soviet Union casting a deciding vote in the United Nations security council. Then I saw it fight for its life against vast numerical superiority. I cheered it along because, I told you, I love helping the underdog in a fight. It gravely disappointed me that decades later, the Israelis forgot the taste of oppression and became occupiers themselves.

I never returned to Russia after that. As the United States and the Soviet Union squared off over Berlin, the Comintern decided to take the struggle to the doorstep of the United States: Central America. I had picked up Spanish during my work with the International Brigade and, at fifty years old, I was one of the more seasoned operatives available. My transfer was arranged directly from the Mideast to Guatemala.

I was involved in many efforts in Central America. There were some real heroes there who were eventually betrayed and eliminated. It was enough to make you give up. But I didn't. I eventually wound up in Cuba, seeing what role I could play. Early on, Fidel didn't want much to do with those of us with Soviet ties. I used this to convince my handlers to cut me loose and let me work as an independent. By now I was nearly sixty and I think they were cutting me loose to die. They didn't know that my parents hadn't made shoddy goods!

In Cuba, I soon met Che and we were immediately attracted to each other. I was attracted to his energy, commitment, endurance and agile mind. I think he was attracted to the fact that I spoke my own mind, not party lines, and not fawning bullshit. We wound up in the Sierra Maestra together and then at the national bank when he returned to Havana and tried to invent a new economic system. In 1962 he asked me, very confidentially, if I would go to Argentina to coordinate a revolutionary beachhead in the northern mountains. I laughed at him. I was nearly sixty-five years old!

It was time for me to go home to the land of my birth, like an elephant returning to her ancestral home for burial. But I had no family left there. I had never married, so there were no hostages who would ensure I'd return (that practice made my blood boil!). If I had, I would probably have changed sides politically and joined the dissidents. I was sick of the oppression. What I call "old revolutionary energy" compared very unfavorably with the young revolutionary energy I had been exposed to now for many years. The party in the Soviet Union had become another bunch of thugs.

Still, I could have stayed in the Americas. The Cuban revolution was new and full of promise. There were wrong things done, but not on the scale that occurred elsewhere. Castro stayed true to his agenda, bringing social welfare to the masses who had been so abused. It is hard to say if he would have evolved a less dictatorial style had not the American government attacked him so relentlessly. Some things we can only guess at. There were also other groups in central and South America that had taken heart from Cuba, some with very good leadership. Why did I go to the United States?

I will tell you the truth if you haven't guessed it. It was a woman. A woman more than ten years younger who took a shine to me! An attractive woman. She was a member of the American Communist Party from Cleveland who had come down to Cuba to see for herself what was going on, violating the shameful travel ban her government had imposed on U.S. Citizens. She came as much to stand up against the ban as to see what was happening in the new world of Cuba – the education, the hospitals, the land reform.

We hung around together in Cuba and things got started between us. When you're well on your way to seventy years old, it is irresistible to have a good-looking woman in her early fifties fall for you. It feels like a stay of execution. She remained in Cuba a few months. When it was time for her to go home and face the music with the US authorities, she made an offer that startled me. Would I like to marry her and come live in the U.S.? Her husband had died a few years earlier. I can't tell you on how many levels this proposition rattled me, and I don't know which level would have registered stronger on the Richter scale.

Marriage? That was nearly a 6.0 by itself. I had lived my whole life outside this institution. To start now? Leave Cuba where I had comrades and friends and go to a strange country in whose language I was then weak and where I knew no one? Go, of all places, to the U.S., which symbolized everything we fought against, and live in the belly of the beast? That was nearly an 8.0!

I also thought it inadvisable for her to add to the woes she would have with her government by bringing home a documentable Soviet agent. I agreed, instead, to first go on a false passport and visa and to stay there for six months before making up my mind about her offer. With the help of the resources to which we had access, I was given papers that wouldn't arouse the suspicions of the Immigration Service. We left on the same flight, appearing to travel separately.

I didn't realize what an exciting time I was walking into in US politics. The civil rights movement to end the despicable apartheid that existed officially throughout the southern states, and unofficially throughout the country, was mobilizing hundreds of thousands of students. Direct activism and confrontation were breaking out everywhere. Bigots were murdering freedom riders and the police were breaking heads of demonstrators. It felt like life had once again favored me with the timing to walk into the beginnings of revolutionary change.

I was wrong, of course, about this. It was not a true revolutionary situation. But I was right that life had favored me. I wound up marrying the woman and securing permanent residency rights in the U.S. I participated in the civil rights struggles, and became even more active as the anti-Vietnam war movement developed. There were times when it seemed to my eyes that the country would explode in violent struggle, but it never did. Pockets of violence flared and extinguished. But what I saw, which I almost couldn't believe, was that change occurred anyway. The American South was officially desegregated and the war in Vietnam was stopped, without overthrowing the U.S. government.

I was no naive cherry and saw clearly that the military-industrial complex still called a lot of the shots, and the plight of U.S. blacks still remained far inferior to their white countrymen. But, the nation had paid a relatively small price in human suffering and had taken significant steps forward as a result of the non-violent activist tactics. When I compared this with the horrendous suffering I had witnessed in revolutionary Russia and China and elsewhere, I was no longer so sure that armed struggle was the necessary and superior philosophy. Nor was I any longer uncomfortable with my adopted country, despite all the things it still had to answer for.

My wife died on my eightieth birthday. She stepped off the curb at a busy intersection and was hit by a reckless taxi driver. It is ironic that one can live through so much violence and lose a loved one stepping off a curb. The modest estate she left has let me live independently. It has allowed me to read all the newspapers I read every day, and the many books I borrow from the libraries. It has let me follow the revolutionary struggles that still exist, only a handful of which I can still admire. As I told you, I have seen too much.

Now you know my story. Maybe you will just conclude that the old man has gone soft and has been duped. Maybe you are right. Maybe not. Maybe the old man has learned a few things. Maybe it pays to at least hear him out.

CHAPTER IV:
Having Won the Revolution

The End Game

When things are going poorly, be brave.
When things are going well, be reflective
- Traditional Korean saying

Ending a revolution is as hard as starting one. Each situation is different. But if you don't get this right, you blow the chance for which you have fought for so long. Or you blow the country apart.

It is so easy to spawn a civil war in the wake of revolution. There are so many parties and interests, so many egos and righteous views, so much anger and fear, so much desperation and greed, and so much ordnance lying around the countryside.

Think of it this way. You have toiled in the vineyard for years doing back breaking work. At last your vines have reached maturity and the fruit is ready to be picked. You can almost taste its delicious flavor bursting in your mouth. But instead of picking the fruit, at this moment you pick fights with the other people in the vineyard, or they pick fights with you. You argue over how to divide up the harvest, who deserves what portion, who will control which sectors, what your titles and positions will be, how the vineyard will be managed, what label will go on its products. Everyone is "on guard." No one gets, at last, to enjoy the fruits of their labor. Worse, fighting breaks out, the main structures of the winery are reduced to rubble, the harvest cannot be processed, the vines catch fire and burn in the last hot days of autumn, land mines in the rows between the vines blow off the legs of the workers and firefighters. No one wins anything of value. The victor presides over scorched earth and moral and economic bankruptcy.

I paint a discouraging picture because I have seen just this occur. I have also seen people drunk with joy when the revolution is brought to a successful conclusion. What makes the difference? You should ask this question yourself. While you are answering it, I'll share with you what I have learned. At the end of my life, that is the most precious thing I have to share.

I have learned that there are certain imperatives at this crucial juncture for the revolutionary leadership. Let me describe how I see them.

The Nation Must Be Preserved

Unless the revolution specifically refutes the legitimacy of the nation, preserving the nation must be a paramount value. This may mean collaborating with factions you don't fully trust, with factions who under war conditions betrayed you, factions whose philosophies are substantially different than yours. This is very, very difficult to do. You have fought Goliath for years and are on the eve of toppling him forever. Why must you now seem to give in to less formidable opponents? You have rolled the dice for years. Why settle for partial victory? Why not roll them one more time and go for the jackpot – total victory?

The answer is precisely because your country is not to be gambled with. It is not your toy or game. Too many suffer when you take to the trenches "one more time." You have become cocky about using military solutions. You cannot continue to use them when there are options for legitimate negotiations. They are the wrong tool for the job. If you continue to reach for this tool, you will come to rely on force of arms as your primary vehicle for getting what you want or what you believe is necessary. But civil society is not built on force of arms. What was legitimate under revolutionary conditions when dialogue and negotiation were not available to you, is no longer legitimate when you have political options. You must retrain and reaccustom yourself to the limits civil society requires.

I was not with Mandela before he went to prison and, to my profound disappointment, I was too old to join him when he was released, or I would have, in a flash! He was an old man, but I was already ancient. The best I could do, when I saw what he was about to achieve, was to study him closely. Who would have predicted South Africa could throw off decades of oppressive government without a massive blood bath? Yet it happened. There is much to learn from their experience.

Look at how Mandela worked with de Klerk, who headed the repressive regime in its final stages, and with Chief Buthelezi whose Inkatha Zulus under right wing goading continued to wage violence against his own African National Congress. He was determined that neither white extremists, who were demanding a white homeland, nor black extremists who opposed negotiations and elections, would be permitted to break up the country.

He continuously extended olive branches when factions in either group maneuvered to block a negotiated resolution. He did not personalize what was occurring. This was not about him or his rivals. This was about the country.

Mandela resisted all attempts to goad him into a divisive response. He held to his principles firmly, but not to his ego. He worked as hard at the final negotiations as he had in the struggle. He understood that they were a part of the struggle, another form of struggle, with its own rules and methods of engagement. He welcomed the struggle rather than railing against it. It was the necessary last stage to bringing all parties into the negotiated settlement, to leaving none outside to snipe at it, to forming a truly different future for his country and its people.

Perhaps most amazing of all, when the right of universal suffrage was finally secured and Mandela's party won a plurality, but not a clear majority, he applauded the outcome while others in the ANC regarded it as a failure. To Mandela's thinking, the lack of an outright majority would ensure that the ANC worked with other parties to fashion a constitution that everyone could live with, rather than being able to force one down the others' throats. The nation would be better served by having hammered out a consensus. This is the mark of a leader who has made the transition from revolutionary to political life.

I know of no leader who played the end game of a revolution better. If I could have traveled to one more country in my life, I would have loved nothing better than to be in South Africa on the days of the first universal voting. I would have gladly spent my last days on earth standing in the long, racially integrated lines that snaked towards the polling booths, as if in a dream of the kingdom of justice having arrived on earth, at least for a few days.

Final Objectives Must Be Clear

There must be absolute clarity on the hierarchy of revolutionary objectives so that, if the time comes when some must be sacrificed in order for others to be realized, this will be done.

It is both childish and lethal to insist on realizing one hundred percent of your objectives at the formal ending of hostilities. If you do happen to realize all of them, you are very fortunate. But it you insist on doing so, your people are very unfortunate. You will most likely plunge them into further years of conflict when the country is already debilitated and exhausted from the struggle. You must be prepared to abandon some objectives, but not the most central objectives of the revolution, and this is why clarity of relative importance is crucial.

I told you about the great Mazzini in my grandfather's time whose cherished goal was the unification of Italy and its freedom from foreign domination. To achieve this he had to forego the goal he held nearly equally dearly of replacing the monarchy with a republic. But he willingly deferred the second goal for the first, knowing that one day it, too, would be realized.

I imagine the same choices confronted the founders of my adopted land. Though many of the "founding fathers" were slaveholders, they were not all entirely callous to their crime. But the establishment of a united republic, free of the yoke of monarchy, came first. They could not achieve this primary goal if they sought to create a second revolution for racial justice at the same time. This terrible choice set the stage for another wrenching war three quarters of a century later, so these choices are not without their price. But, eventually, it permitted both objectives to be achieved.

Fidel had to decide whether to take on the Americans at Guantanamo as part of his revolution. Mandela had to postpone economic justice to first achieve political justice and power.

In what surely must be the last years of my life, I hoped to see one more significant wrong righted. I speak of the Palestinians living for decades in makeshift camps and towns, separated from family and sources of livelihood. I thought, surely, in the last weeks as I wrote this, that Chairman Arafat was on the brink of leading his people out of this quagmire. But, sadly, he could not create consensus on the hierarchy of objectives. Being unable to relinquish any, he achieved none. Perhaps history will give him another chance. Perhaps it won't.

The choices revolutionary leaders are called to make at this delicate stage of their struggle are not only crucial to success or failure, but also often excruciating. It is never easy to give up cherished goals. But I have learned that both life and revolution often require us to give up something important to gain something even more important. When we scale mountains, we must be clear which peak will allow us to continue to see the others and, perhaps one day, to reach them, too.

The Radical Must Lead

The most radical, respected and steadfast of the leaders must be the ones to initiate the compromises that achieve the overriding goals of the revolution. Only they can bring along the rest of the revolution's supporters.

People have suffered and sacrificed too much. They will not easily accept a compromise solution that seems to sell out the souls of their fallen comrades and dead family members. They want their suffering and loss to have meant something, and mean something it must. But it must mean the achievable. If it means the unachievable, then the souls of the fallen will writhe forever in the knowledge of near victory and squandered opportunity.

These leaders must not be bound by their own incendiary words that were appropriate to inciting and waging revolution. They must be willing to contradict their own words in order to be true to achieving what is achievable of their revolutionary objectives. The people around them must understand that the words and deeds appropriate to one stage are not the same for another stage. They are not being sold out. At both stages they are being led.

On the threshold of either victory or stalemate in South Africa, it was the ardent communist, Joe Slovo, who proposed to Mandela that they voluntarily suspend armed struggle in order to create the climate for advancing negotiations. Mandela, who steadfastly refused to disarm until blacks were part of the government that received the relinquished arms, recognized the wisdom of Slovo's proposition. And he recognized the wisdom of Slovo as the messenger of the proposition. No one could accuse this radical leader of being the dupe of the white supremacist government.

But, while the radical must lead in the jockeying for final settlement, they must not capitulate to the demands of the most violent amongst themselves. Leaders must recognize that they are embarking on a difficult transition from armed struggle to political struggle. The most violent have no desire or capacity to make this transition. Whatever their contributions to the armed struggle, they are not suited to lead the transition to political settlement. The leadership must stand as strong against the violent wing of their own movement at this juncture, as they stood against the oppressor.

It is to be fully expected that the most violent will attempt to undermine the final negotiations with provocative acts of terror. These must not be regarded by either of the major negotiating parties as a continuation of the struggle. They are the dying paroxysms of the rabid. These are moments that call for the greatest leadership on each side of the struggle. The radical, responsible, credible leadership on both sides, must rise above the vicious, clever and often disguised tactics of the rabid. They must individually and jointly reject them as the morbid remnants of the old order while they steadfastly create the new order.

This is the last test of leadership before being permitted to enter that new world for which you struggled so long and so arduously. Rise to the test.

Total Surrender Must be Managed

While most revolutions will successfully conclude in some form of negotiated settlement, a few resolve in the complete surrender of the oppressive regime, usually after the flight of its scurrilous leaders. This situation presents its own urgent need for the wise and firm management of events that will unfold explosively before you.

In a negotiated settlement, there is still some balance of power, though greatly tipped in favor of the revolutionaries. Almost always, there are more than one faction on both sides, each of which holds some of this power. The fact that there are strong negotiating partners in the process, restrains and guides the acts of all partners.

If the revolution achieves unconditional surrender and complete power, the restraints are suddenly completely lifted. It as if you were pushing with all your might against the gates to the city when, suddenly, they are flung open. The great force with which you were pushing, catapults you wildly into the city now that there is no counter force.

It is the same with sudden, total victory. There is so much built up energy and emotion and adrenaline fortifying one to fight, that sudden, total victory unleashes great and terrible forces into the streets and countryside, frantic for targets to attack. It is a time in which rampages occur against real and suspected opponents. In which anger and pain boil over and seek out any available outlet. In which the most primitive urges to destroy the vanquished, and to plant the victor's seed in their wives and daughters, break out of the constraints of civil society. The bloodbaths and crimes committed in this sudden vacuum can indelibly imprint themselves into the consciousness of the nation, forever thwarting the goal of reconciliation and unification.

The leadership must move more quickly than it can imagine to channel these forces. It is hopeless to do this by using force against one's own people. In any case, it is the last thing you want to do at this moment of great victory. Nor would your troops implement such orders. The huge crowds that pour into the streets are like a sea. You cannot stand against the sea. You can only hope to channel it. The leadership needed at this acute moment is to find ways of symbolically expressing the newfound power and of channeling the pumping adrenaline so they do not have to be expressed through violent forms of release and nightmarish reigns of terror.

The leadership must gather the people in vast rallies in which the symbols of the repressive regime are destroyed and the symbols of the new order are unfurled. They must lead the massive crowds in rousing chants and exuberant songs and dances. They may march them between locations and edifices of great symbolic importance. They may have them take picks and sledgehammers to the monuments of oppression and take plaster and paint brushes to the temples of freedom. For days they must keep the crowd active and focused, letting their uncontrollable energy express itself in great physical outbursts of nonviolent, non-vigilante activity. All the while, amid the chanting and singing and roaring, they must reiterate that the revolution was always against the oppressive system, not against the people caught in that system and turned into collaborators and agents of that system. There will be time to sort out who were victims and who were aggressors, but that must be done in measured ways once the celebrations are over, through tribunals and commissions. Now is the time to celebrate, not take retribution. Now is the time to revel in the communal victory, not redress individual wrongs. To everything its time.

If, despite these energetic efforts, spontaneous violence erupts against those who sympathized or collaborated with the oppressive regime, the leadership must publicly and unambiguously scold and mourn that violence, not celebrate it. They must begin the process of healing. The ways of violence do not get unlearned overnight. Those who lead the learning of violence in struggle must lead its unlearning in victory.

Though I am not always a fan of the Judeo-Christian bible, or other religious tracts for that matter, in this case the Old Testament provides the best parable for teaching this lesson. Let me retell it to you, in my own words.

Cry For the Drowned

It had been many generations since the Hebrew people had come to the land of Egypt. They multiplied, and threatened to outnumber the Egyptians, even as in our time the Arabs threaten to outnumber the Jews in Israel. The Pharaoh chose to take harsh measures to limit their strength and serve his own economic needs.

He gradually reduced the Hebrews to the status of slaves working on his endless monuments to himself and his gods. When they continued to multiply, he conceived a heinous policy: that all newborn males be put to death. The people wailed in their agony.

One of these condemned babies was rescued by placing him adrift in a basket on the river. While bathing in the river, the hand servants of the Pharaoh's daughter found the infant and showed it to the Princess. A strange mood overcame her. Though she knew why the baby must have been abandoned, she felt drawn to take the child into her own court and raise it as her son.

The baby's older sister had watched all this and cleverly offered the services of her mother as a wet nurse. So the child was not raised without knowledge of his true identity.

When the child, who was named Moses, came of age, a moment of choice presented itself when he came upon of an Egyptian overseer beating a Hebrew slave. In an instinctive act of compassion, he rose up to intervene, but in his righteous anger he struck too hard and killed the man. As a political act, killing an Egyptian in defense of a Hebrew was unexplainable, so Moses fled to the wilderness.

In the wilderness, like so many revolutionaries in their mountains, a new way of thinking was born inside him. We are told this process was the work of God and we will not argue with this interpretation here.

Moses returned to the royal city and found his way to make demands on the Pharaoh for liberation. As is the way of despots, Pharaoh laughed at this "demand" from those who controlled no legions or arsenals.

We are told that the God of the Hebrews at this point intervened with a series of devastating plagues that destroyed the Egyptian economy and terrified its citizenry. When Pharaoh remained unrelenting, this all-powerful God designed a final blow to demoralize the populace and their Monarch. The first-born sons of all Egyptians mysteriously died in the night, in grizzly symmetry to the killing of the Jewish sons. At this point in the sacred myth we are left to wonder what type of god used infants as weapons in his war of liberation. IS THIS A GOD ONE WANTS ANYTHING TO DO WITH?

Mourning the death of his own first-born, the Pharaoh relented and sent Moses a message to take his people out of Egypt. Knowing the shock of his loss would wear off and turn to fury, Moses activated the organization he had carefully built and they prepared the people to flee at first light. So great was their hurry, they had no time to let their bread rise, which is why future generations commemorate their liberation by eating unleavened bread.

The Hebrews fled like any refugees before the threat of war. They carried what little they could and put their old, their young and their sick on the few carts in their possession. Moses urged them on to create as much distance as possible between them and the stables of the Egyptian horses and chariots.

When the numbness began to thaw, the Pharaoh's anger rose in great waves and he screamed for his generals to prepare their animals and men for pursuit. The earth thundered under the hooves, and the clouds of dust the army raised could be seen a day's ride away.

As the signs of the murderous army's approach reached the Hebrews they fell to their knees and lamented they had ever followed the leaders of the rebellion. They would now be cruelly cut down and see their daughters and wives defiled before their dying eyes.

As a wave of fury had spread over Pharaoh, a wave of desperation spread over Moses. It took all the strength of his character and faith to continue to lead in the face of impending disaster. Rallying his lieutenants, he urged the people forward to the sea that lay just hours ahead of them. To what purpose? To be driven into the sea?

But faith and determination often open doors in what seem to be walls. The God of the Hebrews caused the wind to blow in a direction and strength only rarely seen in that place where the waters narrowed to a channel. The waters were pushed aside long enough for the Hebrew leaders to shepherd all of their people to the far side of the channel. As they reached firm footing they turned and saw the vast Egyptian army crest the rise of land on the shore they had just left.

The winds were shifting and the waters began churning back into the channel, still caught between the forces that gripped them. The Egyptian General saw the changing weather pattern and halted his column, determining they would need to suspend the pursuit until barges could be brought to ferry the heavy chariots. But the Pharaoh's fury and arrogance would have none of this. He ordered the General to pursue and, in the way of all autocracies, the General against his good judgment, complied.

While Pharaoh and his personal guard watched from the safety of the shore, the army entered the still exposed seabed, and struggled to keep their heavy chariots moving forward through the sodden sand and gravel, water swirling around their axles. As they reached the middle of the channel, with none of the army's elements on either shore, the wind finished its shift and, with a cataclysmic roar, the waters rushed back into the vacuum. Chariots capsized, horses snarled in their tackle and were dragged to the seabed, men were unable to untie the leather thongs holding their armor in place, and were pulled under, to resurface only days later when their bloated corpses floated onto beaches.

The Hebrews, watching from the far shore, too spent to put any more distance between themselves and their would-be executioners, watched in astonishment as the waters closed over the Egyptians. A great roar of jubilation arose from the throats of the Hebrews. Despite their deep exhaustion they stood and danced and hugged and laughed at the destruction of their enemy. Their freedom was now secure.

As they shouted in joy, the voice of their God spoke to Moses. "Do not let them rejoice with such jubilation, for the Egyptians, too, were my creation."

Moses stood on the highest point of the shore and lifted his arms above his head until some of the revelers became aware of him. They nudged their fellow revelers and the sounds of celebration subsided. A stillness fell over the people, in stark contrast to the din of moments earlier.

Moses conveyed to the Hebrews the instructions he had heard from God. At last they knew this was the kind of God to worship.

The Jews are enjoined, ever since, to tell the story of the exodus from Egypt during their spring celebration of Passover and to remember, indeed, to never forget this lesson. With their index finger they place ten drops of wine from their glass onto their plates to remember the ten plagues and the drowning of the Egyptian army, as both the instruments of their freedom, and the blood that was shed of their fellow human beings.

When Does the Revolution End?

When does the revolution end? It seems such an easy question. As in most things, it is not. The revolution does not end on the day that the oppressor acquiesces. In some ways, that is the day it just begins. But neither does it continue for years or decades after victory.

There is not always a clear line between evolutionary development and revolutionary transformation. When did the revolution actually begin? There is probably a symbolic date, but it is only that. A process of fundamental change began long before that symbolic birth date, picking up momentum until it burst out of the incremental track on which it had run and exploded across the landscape. Similarly, the revolution doesn't neatly end on a certain date. Revolutionary energy continues to drive the restructuring of the old order for some time, but all the while dissipating. At some point, it is no longer recognizable as revolutionary energy and is more readily identifiable as a return to a stable or evolutionary state.

Why is it important to distinguish between these two states?

I have seen this transition period become very confusing for both leaders and their people and give rise to wildly differing expectations. These differences result in unnecessary distrust, suffering, recriminations and doubts. You will do well to avoid or minimize these. As always, I have no magic answers, but offer you some things to pay attention to and consider.

First, let me address the true revolutionary state, which continues to exist for months, and sometimes for a few years after the formal victory, but not longer. All true revolutions depend on the support of the people for their energy and legitimacy. People, like all things in nature, seek a state of dynamic equilibrium. They move toward this like plants toward the sun. They need equilibrium to clear their land, grow their crops, build their homes, educate their families, contemplate their future and implement their plans for arriving there. When they are oppressed too hard, for too long, they are willing, in desperation, to throw away their harsh equilibrium for the promise of a more favorable equilibrium at the conclusion of a revolutionary interval. But be assured, it is equilibrium they will again seek.

So there is a window in which great revolutionary changes can occur, in which laws and power relationships and culture and institutions, and a people's very understanding of the world in which they live, can be fundamentally altered. If the revolutionary leadership has done its job well, it has been preparing the people for these changes before victory itself was secured. But the reality of change always makes a vastly greater impact than its contemplation.

The challenge in this period, and it is a great challenge, is to judge the right amount of change that the system, and the people in it, can tolerate. Doing this has flummoxed every great revolution. Introduce too much change and the system rebels or collapses, causing you to back pedal with great loss of confidence and support. Introduce too little change and you squander the opportunity which you fought so hard to create. I personally have come to believe that you can, and usually should, risk too much change provided you do so with the greatest amount of respect possible for all of those whose lives will be altered by the changes.

I cannot emphasize this point enough. If you force through changes with disdain for the people who are affected and resist your efforts, you will create powerful backlashes. It is not the old order that will be in a position to organize against you, it is the very people you serve!

If the people themselves rise against you, as they did against V.I. and Mao and others, you will be sucked into using the oppressive means of your predecessors against them. You underestimate how well you have learned the ways of those you deplored! The lessons are there, even if they lie dormant, awaiting the conditions to activate them. Instead, you must do what the oppressor never did: have genuine concern for those who bear the brunt of your actions and policies.

This sounds simplistic and it is. I've also come to believe that it is fundamental. From a position of genuine concern, the tactics you adopt will create a climate that permits you to make more changes than you could otherwise make, regardless if you control all the arsenals and radio stations in the country.

All governments use force, implicitly or explicitly, to implement their policies. The difference between oppressive regimes and legitimate regimes is whether you permit people to be brutalized if they stand in your way. Brutality is a common instrument of policy. My own view, after all these decades, is that the true revolution comes about when you adopt a radically different strategy from the age old and, therefore, unrevolutionary strategy of raw intimidation. I now hold the belief that a truly revolutionary strategy relies on consulting the people whose lives will be affected and offering a degree of self-determination within a range of options that honor your revolutionary principles. If you have been listening to the people in whose name you are fighting, the options you propose will address their needs, while protecting the basic needs of the minorities for whom you are also now responsible. You do what must be done but you do not perpetrate widespread injustice and mass terror in doing so.

I know this goes against Che's call for, "injustice at the service of future justice." I know this goes particularly against V.I.'s shockingly bald principle, "The law should not abolish terror... It should be substantiated and legalized clearly, without evasion or embellishment." I am telling you what I have come to believe. You must make your own choices of how you will use power.

In any case, you are still left with the question of when and how does the revolution end?

I have learned one more lesson that I consider absolutely critical. Please listen and consider this carefully. I have learned that it is essential to know what is enough.

You see, all great revolutions want to transform the world. This is what drives their leaders while they are true to the revolution's spirit, and what draws hundreds, then thousands, then millions of adherents to their call. What this desire fails to take into account is this fundamental truth:

Transformation of the world is an eternal process; it will never be complete. Therefore, every revolution must come to understand what transformation it can complete and what transformation must be left for another time and to other leaders.

There is a natural ebb and flow of revolutionary energy. There are cycles of expansion and contraction. People and systems who are challenged will expand and incorporate a significant amount of change within themselves. Then they will contract and take time to digest and assimilate this change and will resist further change while doing so. If revolutionary leadership does not perceive and understand this natural ebb and flow, it will attempt to keep forcing change and will be met with deep, visceral resistance. If the leadership does not recognize "what is enough" it will attempt to overcome this resistance with brute force and, in doing so, will begin to unravel the very revolution it has created.

The revolution must know when it has done what can be done in the window of revolution that it found or created. When the window is closing, it must not force it open as it will only shatter it, leaving broken glass and dreams littering the streets. It must acknowledge and rejoice over what it has been able to accomplish and not become bitter about what it was not able to achieve. All human beings and all revolutions reach a point when they must review their lives and take satisfaction in what they have accomplished, though it often falls short of the fullness of their dreams. They have not failed. They have been true to themselves and they have carried the torch to the next generation.

Let me be clear. I am not saying that they must then stop trying to do anything more with the energy they still possess. I agree with the South African activist who, when asked if the revolution is over said, "If you mean fighting against indifference towards poverty and injustice, "The revolution is forever."

I am saying that they must know when it is time to shift gears and move to a level of expectation and activity appropriate to the stage they have now reached. There is a time to declare the revolution complete at this time. In the same breath, the leader acknowledges what the revolution has not achieved that remains to be achieved and encourages the country to keep working toward the ideals of the revolution. But not in fatigues. Not through revolutionary tribunals. Not with the expediency of revolutionary justice.

Good revolutions are imperfect. Revolutions that demand perfection are evil. They organize witch-hunts and cleansing campaigns and cultures of paranoia and betrayal. They did not start out evil, but become so because they did not understand the principle of "enough." It is enough for this time and place. It will be built on by other like-minded spirits in another time and place. And they, too, will need to know when it is enough, and so on, generation to generation, for as long as human beings strive to leave their mark on the development of the world.

Defections

Let me tell you something strange. Do not fear defections. Learn from them.

First, let's distinguish between defections while you are still fighting the oppressor and defections once you are in power.

While you are engaged in armed struggle there obviously is something to fear from defections, namely breaches of security. In a state of war, these are fatal. Therefore you must pay attention to signs of disgruntlement, and energetically eliminate or reduce the causes when possible. Some causes are inevitable. The recruits could not imagine how difficult the conditions of struggle would be. Others are remedial. Boorish commanders, internal racism, terrible food, numbing inactivity, agent provocateurs. If you cannot effectively remedy the problems, you will need to guard against likely defections. I leave it to you to decide who might pose a threat to security by defecting and what measures are appropriate. But please, don't be paranoid in your assessment, don't exaggerate the dangers. Don't further demoralize your cadres by Draconian acts.

Beyond security risks the subject of defections gets murkier. There is a view that a defection is akin to a military desertion and must be treated as such. There is an uncomfortable injustice about this, as those who showed up to serve you, but fail, are treated more harshly than those who never tried. But war is such a gruesome affair that you only keep people in it by making the penalty for leaving as bad or worse than staying to fight. This becomes a military decision. I suppose you can use military solutions such as defining what a tour of duty is and letting people leave when their current tour is up.

Of course you wish everyone shared your complete commitment to the revolution and its successful conclusion, but not everyone will. If you design exit strategies for those who don't have your unlimited fortitude, they will be less motivated to forge their own wildcat strategies that demoralize and threaten your forces.

Once you are victorious, defections are an entirely different matter. We are no longer talking of defections from the guerrilla force. We are talking of defections from your party, your policies or your country.

Contrary to the common impulse, it a mistake to fear defections or to coercively forbid them. In fact, they provide a crucial source of information on how things are going and what you need to do differently if the political, economic and social revolution is to succeed.

You must understand that people can express their support or resistance to your revolution in two ways. The first is by their voice and actions. The second is by their willingness to stay or their desire to leave. Either of these give you tremendously important information as to whether you are meeting the needs of your people and winning their hearts, or not.

I understand that you may not believe that the people are as yet capable of knowing what they need, of knowing what is good for them. They have internalized the beliefs of the oppressor and still see the world through those distorted eyes. It will take re-education and time to change this. You will throw the story of the flight from Egypt back in my face and tell me that it took forty years of wandering in the desert before the slave mentality was erased from the Hebrew mind and they were ready to enter the Promised Land.

I will agree, and I will argue back. The people do need re-education and new experience and time to digest and assimilate this. They will not magically become the "new" man or woman you believe they are destined to become. But neither will you magically become the "new" enlightened ruler you desire to be. You, too, have deeply ingrained patterns. As much as you aspire to revolutionary consciousness, which I admire greatly, you will still act from old patterns too. This is the tragic flaw in the Leninist insistence on the Revolutionary Vanguard.

Therefore, unless the people have a way to push back, to respond to your initiatives, there is as great a chance that the revolution will go off the rails due to you as it will due to them. Look at the number of post-revolutionary countries that became hellholes! They considerably outnumber the countries that became models of radical progress.

Why? And what is the remedy?

Building a new culture is a dialogue, not a monologue. That you have a vision and had the courage to fight for it does not now entitle you to a monologue! This is where V.I. was a hundred percent wrong. Not because I say so, but because history has proven this. Your victory entitles you to create the conditions for a healthy dialogue, which the oppressive regime never allowed.

The soviet councils that sprung up spontaneously during the revolution were performing just this function. They provided a place for people to express their individual opinions, debate and form consensus on their public opinions and play their role in building the new order. If the revolution had been allowed to truly become a Union of Soviet Socialist Republics it is my belief that it would still be flourishing today and may have allowed the USSR to provide an alternative to the out-of-control consumerist model the US has given the world. Instead V.I. squashed them and became, it pains me to say, a model of revolutionary oppression. .

This dialogue will arise naturally, everywhere, when you are victorious. Allowing it to occur requires the same courage you displayed on the military battlefield. You are now on the battlefield of ideas. Only it shouldn't be a battlefield. It should be an arena in which ideas are contested, not eradicated.

Your success is dependent not just on creating the conditions in which competing ideas can be aired, but in which they are so energetically presented, so vitally compete, are so compellingly drawn, that the entire population pays attention to what is going on in the arena. You have created the conditions that engage their interest and attention, their minds and hearts, so that the process of internal change is accelerated by years and a new consciousness is born.

But you cannot dictate that consciousness. You can parent it. Like a child, it will grow to become its own person. You must let it do this or you will kill or starve it so that it never becomes more than a stunted shadow of its potential.

Doing this requires voices to be heard. You must allow and encourage the diverse voices of human experience to speak up for what you are trying to do and to speak up against what you are doing. This isn't just an exercise in tolerance. This is a great exercise in learning what you need to do to forge a consensus that will bring you closer to the new world you are trying to build.

If you listen, you will learn. If you learn, you will adjust and improve and perfect your message and your policies and your strategies. You will make these corrections until you have found the best attainable balance between what you hope for your people and the realities of the amount of fundamental change they can absorb and assimilate at this point in their evolution. You will have, in fact, found the furthest point of radical change currently achievable without creating the conditions for a devastating backlash. This is your true revolutionary prowess. Aspiring to more than this is revolutionary delusion.

If you do your job well, the best people in your country will stay in the arena and compete to have their vision influence the outcomes of the struggle. The process will remain vibrant and vital. But it is unfair to think that you will do this perfectly. That is the point. None of us are perfect. So intentionally or unintentionally, you will drive some from the arena. You will frighten some off. They will not trust your invitation to speak their minds lest, like Chairman Mao inviting a hundred flowers to bloom, you then use their responses to ferret out the independent thinkers and destroy them.

It is here where defections become a vehicle in their own right.

Some defections should not bother you. They are loyalists to the old regime. They would rather migrate to where they can continue in their old, privileged life style. It is better that they go as they choose to do. Or they have other reasons for which you cannot hold the revolution responsible.

But large numbers of defections should be of great concern. They mean one thing. People are afraid and they do not feel that they have the power to voice their concerns and needs and have them addressed.

What should your revolutionary response be to this? The stupid response is to build a wall around them, deny them visas and shoot them in the back if they attempt to escape. What have you become? The oppressor.

The appropriate revolutionary response requires even greater courage than on the battlefield. It is the courage to hold up a mirror and look at yourself. What are you doing that is creating or contributing to the conditions in which you must forcibly hold people in their own country? People hate to leave their homeland. Living there must be intolerable.

This is cause for the deepest self-examination. There will be terrible internal pressure to say "screw the traitors!" and come down on them with even harsher restrictive measures. I warn you! That is the end of your revolution! And it is not a successful end. This is the moment when you must be greatest of all and ask the simple question: "What mistakes have we made?" and allow non-orthodox answers to that question. Self-correction is greatness.

But do not now make the same error in disguise. If, by fiat, you created the conditions that caused large defections, do not attempt by fiat to correct these. Fiat is the heart of the error. Instead, involve your people in the dialogue to correct the mistakes. Propose changes and ask for corroboration. Ask for their voices. Their views. Teach them that speaking up is again a viable alternative to defection.

And then, take the hardest step. Create the conditions in which you cannot arbitrarily reverse yourself. It will only take one reversal to cause everyone to shut up for good. From then on they will only work at defection or for your overthrow. Instead, create the mechanisms to limit revolutionary power and embed the mechanisms for change into the civil or clerical institutions you create. Replace forever both the oppressive regime and the revolution, with the synthesis that embraces the voices of the governed.

If you do your job well, defections disappear as an issue. You will have created the conditions in which people want to flock to your country rather than flee it. If you have done your job well, they will use their voices to carry on the work you began and to honor the great thing you have done for them.

Building a New World:
Changing the Structure, Maintaining the Spirit

Transcriber's Note

> Élan did not finish this chapter. See the epilogue and post-epilogue for explanation. He did leave some notes. But he did not expound on these as he did for the previous chapters. Rather than put words in his mouth that may not reflect his intention, I have chosen to simply arrange the notes and present them as I found them. The very last chapter that appears in the table of contents was not even outlined so I have left it as a chapter heading without a body.

Post Victory: Building New World.

Three Factors:

1. Revolutionary Spirit

2. Political and Administrative Institutions

3. Satisfying Needs of People

Three factors must be juxtaposed/balanced.

Revolutionary spirit:

People excited about change. Possibilities. Want to participate. Don't be afraid. Find ways to encourage. Workers' councils. Student Councils. Others. They will organize themselves. Stay out of the way. Don't block. Don't control. Channel energy.

Political/Administrative institutions:

Don't neglect or delay. Don't rely on revolutionary instruments for long. Set up civil instruments. Don't use excuses. Separate political and administrative institutions. Religious institutions, too, if applicable. Different types of people good at different functions. Political love debate and competition. Administrative love hierarchy and order. Clerical should love morality and first principles.

Political:

Be brave. Distribute power. Anything else guarantees future oppression. Reexamine ideology that says otherwise. Give each group some real power. They have better chance of holding each other in check. Don't worry about one person or group having too much power. Power needed to get things done. Make sure all groups have sufficient power to compete and balance. Define the political agenda based on revolutionary goals. Don't fear debate and modification. Builds support. Keep the focus on goals. Keep yourself in reserve if they stray too far from goals. Appeal to people to refocus debate and demand action.

Administrative:

Seek competent technocrats. People who can make trains run on time. Who understand finance, labor, production, distribution, users, interagency cooperation. Crack down hard on first signs of cronyism or corruption. Put own people in places they can monitor what's going on in bureaucracy. Don't get blindsided. Don't relax or let others relax. Be fair and tough.

Clerical:

To the degree in your power, support leaders who love salvation more than damnation. Uplifting lights vs. polices of orthodoxy. Good sense of division between spiritual and temporal authority.

Satisfying needs of people:

Desperate necessity will overwhelm revolution. Take dramatic steps to address most desperate needs while building political and administrative institutions. Don't neglect either. If possible, push through land and wealth sharing now without driving off those who make economy work. Don't wait till post revolution period. Sharing vs. total confiscation. Partial redistribution. Everyone vested interest in success. Sell it vs. imposing it.

Be everywhere checking on implementation.

Process:

Try, learn, modify, communicate.

Try learn, modify, communicate.

Repeat.

Architecture:

Structure/Spirit/Needs.

Structure/Spirit/Needs.

Balance.

Endings

There comes a time when all your journeys must be inward,
When all your farewells must be forever.
There comes a time when all "good-nights" mean "good-bye"
When all "thank yous" must carry sufficient weight to never need
repeating.

There comes a time when the darkest does not precede the dawn
When there will not be the chance to wish the world "good-morning."
There comes a time when justice can no longer be served
When it is too late to right wrongs, committed or received.

There comes a time when the past is all there is for us
The future is what is left for others.
There comes a time when the dawn upon the ocean
Will be seen only by other marveling eyes.

There comes a time when the pen runs dry
The lips form no shapes, the chamber is empty.
Write your goodbye notes now. Whisper forgivenesses
and declarations of love. Fire the last round accurately.

Then lie down and close your eyes
Imagine a world you have never seen.
Step into this world like a sky diver
And trust yourself to the eternal wind.

Keeping the Spirit Alive
in Future Generations

Transcriber's Note

This is the chapter that sorrowfully Élan not even outlined. It's your task to learn and teach how to keep the revolutionary spirit alive.

EPILOGUE

If you have read this far you must feel that I am your friend, your supporter. The truth is that I do not know if I support your revolution. I would have to evaluate a lot of information before I made that decision. Remember, I have seen too much.

I would have to know how repressive the regime you are opposing has been. I would have to understand how open or closed are the mechanisms for change. I would have to understand the complexity of racial and tribal conflict in your region. I would need to know the strategies available to you and which ones you are choosing. What suffering you are alleviating and causing, and how these balance. The complexity of motives of your leaders. Your vision for a better world and the values that will guide its attainment. I would want to know how you use your power and how you guard against its abuse.

So, though I have great compassion for revolutionary causes, do not confuse me as necessarily being one of your supporters. You know already that I have come to believe that armed violence must be considered a last resort. That, far too often, it is kept going by those who have something to profit from it: arms merchants, business interests, feuding families, "enemies of my enemy". Too often it becomes an addiction, a diet that cannot be broken despite the terrible costs it inflicts on innocent people.

But know this: if you are striving against oppression, to reduce human suffering and to create opportunities for a better and more free life, I support your intentions and admire your commitment. I will need to trust that you yourself are asking the questions I would ask before supporting or continuing to support the methods you are using.

A revolutionary is someone willing to experience and create great change. Sometimes the appropriate change is in your relation to the revolution itself, what you demand of it, what you will tolerate from it. As you have discovered if you read this far, I believe that to make the revolution worth fighting and dying for, you must always be willing to question the revolution itself. You must not be more lenient in your assessment of its faults than you are in the faults of the regime you are fighting. Your love for the revolution must not blind you to its practices.

I will tell you an experience I had late in life.

I had talked my way into becoming one of the volunteer guides who show people around the Capitol of my adopted country. I got a big kick out of this. If they only knew who I was and what I had done in my life! Anyway, I enjoyed the opportunity of meeting different people and finding out what they believed.

I had been asked to escort a group of legislators visiting from Thailand on a tour of the United States Naval Academy in Annapolis, Maryland. (Imagine that!) I sat between the interpreter and a young man named Burirak in the van which took us to Annapolis. When I met Burirak he was twenty-nine years old. There was a sparkle in his eyes that attracted me.

Burirak was the youngest delegate. I found that he had spent five years in the hills as a guerilla. After five years, for reasons he did not have time or language to fully explain, he had decided that the revolutionary movement was not the way to change things. With the agreement of his commander, he walked out of the hills and re-entered society. He still felt a kinship with his former comrades and did not betray them, but embarked on a new path for reform.

He decided he would run for a seat in parliament and went about the task with all the energy and determination with which he had pursued revolutionary goals in the hills. He tirelessly walked the district that he was campaigning to represent and spoke to everyone he could about their fears and aspirations. To the surprise of nearly everyone in the power structure, he won the seat handily.

The group was now touring other parliaments to glean ideas on how to strengthen their own. It was no secret that control of the government lay largely with the military and that the parliament was still a democratic fig leaf covering the military's naked power. Only a wildly popular hereditary monarch kept the military's brute force in check.

We picked up a naval officer at Annapolis, since the rank of this group warranted an official escort, and began the tour. After a lot of looking at the superficial and glitzy symbols of the Academy's role and achievements, we entered the small and functional dormitory of a new plebe, or officer candidate. Members of the group asked unimportant questions, more to be polite than out of real interest.

Then Burirak asked a question. It seemed simple and innocent. "How are candidates for the Academy selected?" The naval officer proceeded to explain that each year the President of the United States can nominate 100 candidates. The rest of the incoming class of well over 1000 freshman were nominated by members of Congress.

Burirak's eyes widened! "Members of parliament select most of the future officer candidates?"

"Yes" the officer reassured him. "The same with West Point where army officers are trained, and for the air force academy."

Burirak turned to me with a great smile and, gesturing with the extended pointer finger on his right hand, said "Important idea number one! Future military officers appointed by elected members of parliament!"

I smiled back at him, my old eyes twinkling almost as much as his young eyes. He had gone straight to the heart of the matter. A simple tradition, of which most Americans were unaware, created the potential of a military loyal and answerable to an elected parliament, rather than it calling the shots with the executive. Of course this was imperfect, as all of us who have witnessed the misuse of American military might in Central America, the Caribbean and Asia know. But he was right, nevertheless. It provided a framework for changing the power relationships.

We asked further questions and found that the farsighted tradition was instituted, as were so many others, by that distant revolutionary, Thomas Jefferson, another imperfect man and slaveholder who, nevertheless, struck blows for greater equality and freedom, and provided inspiration for San Martin and Bolivar.

Burirak opened my eyes further that day to the many paths to social and political change. And I can still see the sparks in his eyes, which are the igniters of change.

I tell you this story not to dissuade you from your current path but to remind you that you have choices. At any given point you should choose the revolution because it is the best path. If it does not meet that standard at any point, you must have the courage to choose another path. The revolution is not an end. It is a vehicle. It must serve the worthy end that it seeks better than other paths if it is to merit you following it.

Whatever path you choose, I wish you success in achieving your goals for the betterment of the lives of the people for whom you care and fight. Your sacrifices are great. May your rewards be equal.

TRANSCRIBER'S EPILOGUE

Élan wrote the ending poem and the epilogue before we had half finished the book. He was always afraid of dying before completing the work, so he took pains to make his closing points early.

I am sorry to inform you that his fears were realized. As a result, we did not write the final chapters we had agreed to when we outlined the last section. I have chosen to leave them in the table of contents. Perhaps you will want to think about them yourself.

I am very pleased that we were able to nearly complete the book, as I believe in the importance of this work. While Élan was always concerned about not being able to complete the book, a qualitative change occurred in his expression of these fears when he was dictating the final section. I say dictating. I really mean describing. He would leave it to me to organize and put the polish on the words, though I stayed as true to his language as I could.

He began to talk of Lenin's death and how horrible it must have been to have had seven strokes in a few months and lose control of virtually all his faculties. And this at 52! I noticed that in the midst of great lucidity he would, for the first time in our relationship, occasionally lapse into confusing sentences and bits of the first languages he spoke as if he himself were experiencing strokes.

When he talked about Lenin he seemed more forgiving than he had been in earlier analyses of his faults and errors. At one point he said "Poor Vladimir Ilyich! Of course he made mistakes! Look at him – he only lived to half my age! I've had two lifetimes to learn, to his one! Of course I can see his mistakes, especially with the benefit of a half century to see their consequences."

Then he would say, "I don't want to die like V.I. I don't want anyone to have to care for me for months and not be able to even tell them what I need! I don't want that. I want it to be fast. I wish the book were finished, but even if it can't be, I want to go fast."

A few days before his death he told me a strange story. It was a story he had read when he was still middle aged, though he could not remember the author.

A man who was in the twilight of his life sat on the veranda of his home, apparently a large home with extensive gardens. In the distance were gently rolling hills, covered in thick meadow grass. He enjoyed sitting on the veranda, taking in the timeless beauty of his piece of the earth.

Every few days an army would appear on the horizon and begin coming over the hills. It was not clear who this army was, but it was clear that it brought with it death. The man would rise from his chair and go to his garden which was filled with delicate glass flowers. Crystal flowers. He would break off a flower at the stem and listen to the "plink" it made. At the moment he did so, the army would retreat over the hills and disappear beyond the horizon from which it had come. This event repeated itself every few days.

Eventually, there were only a handful of flowers left in the garden. As these were glass flowers they did not renew themselves. The man wistfully realized that he could only turn the army back a few more times. Then there would be nothing to stop its advance and it would swallow up him and his world.

"It is strange" Élan said. "You would think, given all the years I spent as a revolutionary, that I would identify with the army in that story! They persisted despite setback after setback. Victory was finally within their grasp! But I find myself identifying with the man, despite the fact that he is clearly privileged. The world that he loves is about to end and he is powerless to forestall that, just as I am powerless now."

After a long silence with his eyes closed he looked up at me again. "I suppose that he and I were both fortunate to have had our world for as long as we did. I don't know where those glass flowers came from, the story never explains that, but I seemed to have had some of them in my life as well. It's an honor to have lived a century and to have seen so many brave and imperfect men and women try to bring about a more perfect world. I did a little bit to help. That's all we can ask of ourselves. Do a bit."

He was silent again. Then, just when I thought he had fallen asleep, he looked at me again and said, "I learned a few things. I just want to share these." Then he did fall asleep.

For the next ninety-six hours he slept most of the time. He had stopped taking food and only asked for his lips to be moistened a few times. On one of the last times he woke he said in a raspy voice, "Finish it as best you can." Then, "Harper's Ferry. Scatter me there."

It fell to me to carry out his last request. There were no relatives. His peers had all died before him. A couple of fifty and sixty year old lefties from the civil rights and peace movements, who still identified with revolutionaries, accompanied me on this ritual I felt it necessary to perform as we drove to Harper's Ferry in West Virginia, carrying the simple urn. Élan had always felt that the greatest revolutionary act in the land in which he spent his last years, was the raid by the abolitionist John Brown on the Harper's Ferry arsenal. Like so many others revolutionaries, Brown had apparently failed. He was hanged for the raid and his plan to lead slaves in an armed uprising. But had he failed? Not from the long view of history.

We each took a turn scattering ashes over the steep bluffs and watched a light breeze blow them across the river below. I cast the petals of a single red flower along with the ashes. The petals followed the breeze and marked the spot in the river where the ashes had settled. We watched for as long as we could discern the petals on the river as it carried the ashes towards the sea.

What I learned from Élan is that one only fails by not living in a way that shows deep respect for life. The very last time Élan spoke, I believe he spoke to you. He said, "Tell them I love them."

PRINCIPLES

These principles are distilled from Élan's writing:

1. Value transformation over power.
2. Determine the necessary force to realize transformation; no more, no less.
3. Honor individual lives in the pursuit of all life's betterment.
4. Respect comrades who disagree with you; they are still comrades.
5. Learn how to do things better; admit mistakes and stay human.
6. You are not the revolution.
7. You are the symbol of the revolution; live up to it.
8. Do not expect others to behave as symbols.
9. The revolution will be imperfect.
10. Imperfection is preferable to tyranny.
11. Do not become the tyrant in the name of perfection.
12. The revolution will change; accept it.
13. The revolution is in the hearts of people.
14. Hearts are changed over time. Be patient. Persist.
15. The revolution fosters the legitimate interests of all constituencies.
16. Revolution is against illegitimate interests, not against their bearers.
17. At the right time, exchange the revolution for the institutions and practices that will sustain its achievements.

18. Legacies are determined by successfully institutionalizing the legitimate aspirations for which you fought.

19. Only you can ruin your legacy.

20. The legacies of leaders that use power wisely are the threads that weave a just future.

Final Thought
Is Élan an historical figure,
a composite or an ideal?

I prefer to leave this adjudication to you.